My Mediterranean Kitchen

My Mediterranean Kitchen

Mary Valle

NEW HOLLAND

In memory of my mother Katina (1939-2003)

and my father Kosta (1931-2004)

This edition published in 2014 by
New Holland Publishers
London • Sydney • Auckland
www.newhollandpublishers.com

Unit 114, 50 Westminster Bridge Road London SE1 7QY United Kingdom
1/66 Gibbes Street Chatswood NSW 2067 Australia
218 Lake Road Northcote Auckland New Zealand

A catalogue record of this book is available at the British Library and the National Library of Australia.

ISBN: 9781742576114

Publisher: Fiona Schultz
Publishing director: Liane Clarke
Project editor: Jodi De Vantier
Cover designer: Tracy Loughlin
Designers: Tracy Loughlin, Stephanie Foti
Photographer: Graeme Gillies
Food stylist: Stephanie Souvlis
Cook assistants: Rebecca and Sarah Valle
Production director: Olga Dementiev
Printer: Toppan Leefung Printing Ltd

10 9 8 7 6 5 4 3 2 1

Follow New Holland Publishers on
Facebook: www.facebook.com/NewHollandPublishers

Contents

Introduction

My first kitchen was small and did not have the latest oven or any stylish gadgets. The pantry was tiny and there wasn't a lot of cupboard space. The work top had enough room for a toaster and, like my mother, I too would have a small Greek Orthodox icon sitting in a corner, where I would light a small candle on special days. My one indulgence was a bouquet of fresh flowers, usually roses as they are my favourite. The tiles were a retro orange, which I grew to love. We had a small rectangular table, which usually had one of my mother's hand-embroidered tablecloths on it, four chairs around it and, of course, a child's high chair. You couldn't imagine seeing a photograph of this kitchen in the latest design magazines but it was my kitchen, a place where many meals were prepared and many happy memories were made. So, even though I still have visions of my dream kitchen, I would never have changed my first small, not very stylish but cosy kitchen.

As a mother, when I look back I want to know that I did the very best I could, and for me, that includes knowing my family eats well. I do confess that there are times when I feel that I have been cooking forever and that is okay.

For me, home cooking is about dishes that are not complicated or clever but delicious and nutritious in the simplest way...knowing what is in every meal that you have prepared. I cherish the intimacy of the family table, sharing meals I have prepared with love and soul for the people whom I love.

I have a passion for Mediterranean food and especially Greek food as it is what I know best. For the people of the Mediterranean region food represents a way of life...meals are made using the freshest, seasonal produce, prepared simply and shared with family and friends.

Food has the ability to stir up many emotions. It can take you back to your childhood, remind you of a shared dinner with a special someone or a place that you have visited. The recipes in this book are all meals that I prepare for my family, many favourites. I hope that you make these recipes your own and that you are not afraid to add your personal touch...have some fun with them and enjoy!

Mary x

My Pantry

Olive oil—everyday cooking olive oil and
   for salads
Rice
   for paella—short grain rice. There is
   one called 'bomba', which is great, but
   you can also use short- or medium-
   grain rice.
   risotto rice—I like to use Carnaroli
   medium-grain rice—for sweets and
   stuffings
   basmati rice or long-grain—for pilaf
Pasta
   fresh and dry (fresh keeps for only a
   few days in the refrigerator) spaghetti,
   penne, angel hair and any other
   variety that you love
Bread
Grains
   semolina, couscous, bulghur wheat
Tomato passata, tomato paste and cans
   of diced tomatoes
Flour—self-raising (self-rising), plain (all-
   purpose) and Tipo 00 (super-fine)
Yogurt—I recommend Greek yogurt, but
   any natural (plain), creamy yogurt will
   do.

Pulses—lentils, cannellini (white) beans
   (both dried and in cans), chickpeas
   (garbanzo beans)
Vanilla extract
Vinegar—red wine, white wine and
   balsamic
Sea salt
Black peppercorns and a grinder
Sugar—caster (superfine) and icing
   (confectioners')
Filo pastry
Olives
Cheese—feta, mozzarella, fresh ricotta,
   parmigiano
Honey
Eggs
Garlic, onions, lemons, potatoes
Dried herbs and spices—basil, bay
   leaves, cinnamon (ground and sticks),
   cloves (ground and whole), fennel
   seeds, nutmeg, oregano, rosemary,
   saffron, sesame seeds, sweet paprika,
   tarragon

Seasonal Fruit, Vegetables and Herbs

Summer

apricots, avocado, bananas, basil, beans, beetroot, berries, capsicum (bell peppers), carrots, cherries, cucumber, eggplant (aubergine), figs, grapefruit, grapes, leeks, lettuce, melons, nectarines, onion, parsley, passionfruit, peaches, pears, peas, pineapple, plums, potatoes, spring onions, sweet corn, tomatoes, zucchini (courgettes).

Winter

apples, artichokes, bananas, beetroot, blood oranges, broccoli, Brussels sprouts, cabbage, carrots, cauliflower, celery, kumquat, garlic, grapefruit, kiwi fruit, leeks, lemons, lettuce, lime, mandarins, onions, oranges, parsley, pineapple, potatoes, silverbeet, snow peas (mange tout), spinach.

Autumn

bananas, beans, beetroot, cabbage, capsicum (bell peppers), carrots, cauliflower, celery, chestnuts, cucumber, eggplant (aubergine), fennel, figs, grapefruit, grapes, leeks, lettuce, mandarins, melons, mushrooms, nuts, onions, parsley, pears, peas, plums, pomegranates, potatoes, pumpkin, quince, sweet corn, sweet potato, tomatoes, zucchini (courgettes).

Spring

artichokes, asparagus, bananas, basil, beans, beetroot, berries, broad beans, broccoli, capsicum (bell peppers), carrots, cauliflower, chives, cucumber, garlic, grapefruit, leeks, lemons, limes, mandarins, mangoes, onions, parsley, peas, spinach, sweet corn, zucchini (courgettes).

Soups

This is a very simple but very tasty soup, perfect with some fresh crusty bread.

Tomato and Basil Soup

In a large pan, sauté the onions and garlic in a little olive oil until softened. Add the chopped tomatoes and combine. Add 1 litre (1¾ pints, 4 cups) of water, the tomato paste and sugar, and stir well. Season with the salt and pepper and add the basil.

Simmer for about 30 minutes. Pour into bowls, sprinkle with the saved basil leaves and serve immediately with fresh crusty bread.

Serves 4–6

1 onion, finely diced
1 garlic clove, finely diced
olive oil
1 kg (2 lb 4 oz) ripe tomatoes, peeled, seeded and chopped
1 tablespoon tomato paste (concentrate)
2 teaspoons sugar
salt and pepper, to taste
½ cup basil, chopped, reserving a few leaves to sprinkle over the soup before serving

The aroma of Greek coffee still reminds me of my father.

My father was a quiet man with principles. He did not like to be fussed over and took pleasure in the simple things in life. Nothing was more important to him than his girls—my mother, my sister and myself. Of course, as grandchildren came along they also joined that group.

They loved Papou.

Lentil soup is a classic Greek dish. I have added macaroni to this recipe to make it a little more hearty.

Lentil Soup with Macaroni

1 onion, finely diced

1 garlic clove, finely diced

olive oil

350 g (12 oz) brown lentils,
    washed and dried

1 x 400 g (14 oz) can diced
    tomatoes

1 teaspoon sugar

1 bay leaf

100 g (3½ oz) small macaroni

2 tablespoons parsley, chopped

1 tablespoon red wine vinegar

salt and pepper, to taste

Sauté the onions and garlic in a little olive oil in a large pan until softened but not coloured.

Add the lentils, tomatoes, sugar and bay leaf. Pour in about 1.5 litres (2¾ pints, 6 cups) water and bring to boil.

Simmer for about 30 minutes and then add the pasta. Continue cooking for another 10–15 minutes, or until the pasta is cooked.

Add the parsley and vinegar, then season to taste. Serve hot.

Serves 4–6

I adore the flavour of the chorizo in this soup and, because I like a little heat, I have also added some smoked paprika.

Bean, Vegetable and Chorizo Soup

In a large pan, sauté the onion and garlic in a little olive oil over medium heat, until soft.

Drain the beans and add to the pan , then pour in about 1 litre (1¾ pints) of water. Add the tomatoes, tomato paste, sugar and bay leaf and stir well.

Add the vegetables and bring to the boil. Simmer for 30 minutes, then add the chorizo and paprika. Continue cooking for another 30 minutes, or until the beans are cooked.

Season to taste and add the parsley. Serve hot.

Serves 4–6

1 onion, finely diced

1 garlic clove, finely diced

1 tablespoon olive oil

400 g (14 oz) dried butter (lima) or cannellini (white) beans, soaked overnight in a bowl of cold water

1 x 400 g (14 oz) can diced tomatoes

1 tablespoon tomato paste (purée) (concentrate)

1 teaspoon sugar

1 bay leaf

2 carrots, peeled and diced

2 zucchini (courgettes), diced

2 celery stalks, chopped

1 potato, peeled and diced

1 chorizo, chopped into chunks

½ teaspoon smoked paprika (optional)

salt and pepper, to taste

1 tablespoon fresh parsley, chopped

This wholesome, chunky soup takes a little time to prepare but it is worth it. Variations of this soup can be found across the Mediterranean and this is the way I like to make it.

Fisherman's Stew

1 brown onion, sliced

1 tablespoon olive oil

3 celery stalks, sliced

2 garlic cloves, finely diced

3 tomatoes, peeled and
   chopped

3 potatoes, chopped into
   chunks

3 carrots, sliced

2 bay leaves

450 g (1 lb) snapper fillets

1 heaped tablespoon parsley,
   chopped

1 lemon

FOR THE STOCK

1 small whole fish, snapper
   or other firm-fleshed fish,
   cleaned

1 garlic clove

6 black peppercorns

salt

To make the stock, put the fish in a large pan and cover with about 1.5 litres (2¾ pints, 6 cups) of water. Add the garlic clove and season with salt and add peppercorns. Bring to the boil and simmer for 30 minutes. Drain and discard the garlic, peppercorns and bones, but keep the stock and fish flesh.

In a large pan, sauté the onions in a little olive oil. Add the celery, garlic and tomatoes and cook until soft, about 4 to 5 minutes. Add potatoes, carrots and bay leaves and season well. Add 1 litre (1¾ pints, 4 cups) of the fish stock, (making up the volume with water if there isn't quite enough) and simmer gently for 30 minutes. Add the fish fillets and the flesh retained from the stock and simmer for another 20 minutes. When cooked, remove some of the potatoes from the soup and mash them then return them to the soup and mix well.

Add the parsley and a squeeze of lemon. Serve hot in bowls with fresh crusty bread.

Serves 4–6

I have a fondness for one-pot meals, and minestrone, an Italian classic, is one of those. It does not have to be a winter-only soup. Depending on the season in which you are preparing it, you can adjust the vegetables you use.

Minestrone

In a large pan, sauté the onions and garlic in a little olive oil until soft. Add the vegetables, tomato paste and the can of diced tomatoes and combine.

Add 2.5 litres (4½ pints, 10 cups) water and bring to the boil. Add the bay leaf and sugar. Simmer for about 30 minutes. Add the pasta and drained beans and continue cooking for another 15–20 minutes. If the soup starts to look too thick, add some more water.

Season with salt and pepper and add the basil.

Serve sprinkled with Parmesan.

Serves 4–6

1 red onion, finely diced
1 garlic clove, finely diced
1 tablespoon olive oil
2 carrots, diced
1 celery stalk, thinly sliced
2 zucchini (courgettes), diced
1 potato, peeled and diced
200 g (7 oz) spinach, washed and chopped
1 tablespoon tomato paste (purée) (concentrate)
1 x 400 g (14 oz) can diced tomatoes
1 bay leaf
½ teaspoon sugar
100 g (3½ oz) small pasta such as ditalini
1 x 400 g (14 oz) can borlotti beans
½ cup basil leaves
fresh Parmesan, for grating (shredding)

When I travel, the one thing I always love to do, no matter where I am, is to visit the local market. It is one of life's pleasures to wander around fruit or flower stalls, see the amazing array of spices on display, visit the noisy seafood markets—the exquisite and colourful local seasonal produce on show seems endless and I know I will always leave with some small purchase.

This dish is perfect as a mezze or as a side to a meat dish.

Leek and Celery Avgolemono

3 leeks, trimmed, washed,
    halved lengthways and sliced
    into 4 cm (1¾ in) pieces
6 stalks celery, trimmed,
    washed and sliced in 4 cm
    (1¾ in) pieces
1 tablespoon olive oil
salt and pepper, to taste
Egg and Lemon Sauce (see
    Salads)
1 tablespoon dill, chopped

Sauté the leeks and celery in a little olive oil in a large pan. Season with salt and black pepper. Pour in a little water, about 125 ml (4 fl oz, ½ cup) should be enough, and simmer until cooked.

Turn the heat off and prepare the egg and lemon sauce.

Pour the sauce over the leeks, sprinkle with dill and shake the pan to combine.

Serve hot or warm with fresh crusty bread, as a starter or as a side to grilled (broiled) meats.

Serves 4–6

Starters and Sides

Bruschetta is the perfect mezze—magnificent ripe tomatoes with the best olive oil on a slice of bread, and because I love a Greek salad, this is my Greek-style Italian bruschetta.

Greek-Style Bruschetta

Put the cucumber, red onio and tomato dice in a bowl. Add the olives and oregano. Drizzle a little olive oil over the salad and season to taste.

Grill (broil) the bread lightly and then spoon some salad onto each slice. Top with some crumbled feta and serve immediately.

Serves 4 as a side

*1 small cucumber, peeled and
   diced*
*1 small red onion, peeled and
   diced*
2 tomatoes, seeded and diced
150 g (5 oz) pitted black olives
*1 tablespoon oregano, finely
   chopped*
1 tablespoon olive oil
salt and pepper
8 thickly cut slices of bread
*150 g (5 oz) feta cheese,
   crumbled*

A frittata is perfect when you need a quick nutritious meal. I often use bottled roasted red capsicum for this dish together with the chorizo to ensure the frittata will be full of flavour.

Frittata with Chorizo and Roasted Red Capsicum

1 tablespoon olive oil

1 large potato, diced

1 red onion, diced

100 g (3½ oz) chorizo, sliced

1 roasted red capsicum (bell pepper), sliced into strips

50 g (1¾ oz) feta cheese, crumbled

6 large eggs

1 tablespoon parsley, chopped

salt and pepper, to taste

In a large, deep frying pan or skillet (that can be placed under the grill/broiler), heat the olive oil. Sauté the potato in the oil for about 4 minutes, until soft. Add the onion and chorizo and sauté for another 2 minutes, or until onion is soft. Add the capsicum and crumbled feta.

In a large bowl, beat the eggs using a fork. Add the parsley and season well.

Pour over the vegetable mixture. Cover and cook over medium heat for 2–3 minutes, or until the frittata is almost set.

Place under the grill (broiler) for another 2 minutes, or until golden brown.

When cooked, allow to cool a little then loosen the sides and slide onto a plate.

Cut into wedges and serve.

Serves 4

Whether it is for breakfast, a light lunch or Sunday night dinner, an omelette can be made to order. This is one of my favourites.

Omelette with Feta, Tomato and Mint

Melt the butter and the oil together in a large frying pan over medium heat.

Break the eggs into a bowl and lightly whisk using a fork. Whisk the milk into the eggs and pour the mixture into the pan.

Place the tomato onto one half of the egg mixture. Top with the feta, mint and seasoning.

As the egg mixture begins to set, fold the other half of the omelette over the tomato mixture using a spatula. Cook until the omelette has set, then slide onto a plate.

Serve immediately.

Serves 2

25 g (¾ oz) unsalted butter
1 tablespoon olive oil
4 eggs
60 ml (2 fl oz, ¼ cup) milk
1 tomato, diced and seeded
75 g (2½ oz) feta, crumbled
salt and pepper, to taste
1 tablespoon mint, chopped

I love the comforting combination of potato and eggs and it seems that each country has their own variation on how they put these two together. The Spanish omelette is perfect.

Spanish Omelette

75 ml (2½ fl oz, ⅓ cup) olive oil

4 large potatoes, peeled and sliced into 5 mm (¼ in) rounds

2 large onions, peeled and sliced

6 eggs

salt and pepper, to taste

Pour the olive oil into a deep frying pan set over medium heat and heat until hot. Add the potatoes and onions and, turning occasionally, heat until they are cooked through, about 10–12 minutes. Pour out any excess oil from the frying pan.

Meanwhile, in a large bowl, beat the eggs using a fork and season well.

Pour the egg mixture over the potatoes and onions and continue to cook over medium heat. When the omelette sides are cooked, slide it onto a plate and then place the frying pan over the plate. Flip the plate, pan and omelette over and return the omelette to the pan to cook the other side. Fry until golden.

Serve hot or warm.

Serves 4

I remember walking home from school, my mother meeting me halfway with my sister in the stroller. She always carried a sweet biscuit with her for me to eat on the walk home.

These nostalgic memories are the ones I keep close to my heart.

Bulghur Pilaf

In a large pan, melt the butter and sauté the onion until softened. Add the bulghur wheat and stir to combine, then add the liquid. Season to taste and simmer for about 15 minutes, or until the bulghur is cooked.

Fluff up the bulghur using a fork and add the parsley and mint. Serve with meat or chicken dishes with a bowl of yogurt on the side.

Serves 4 as a side

20 g (¾ oz) butter

1 small onion, peeled and finely diced

350 g (12 oz, 2 cups) bulghur wheat, rinsed

750 ml (24 fl oz, 3 cups) chicken stock or water

salt and pepper, to taste

1 teaspoon parsley, finely chopped

1 teaspoon mint, finely chopped

natural (plain) yogurt, to serve (optional)

This plain pilaf can be served with a rich tomato sauce or on its own as an accompaniment to meat and seafood dishes. It also goes well with some vegetable dishes.

Plain Pilaf

20 g (¾ oz) butter

1 small onion, finely diced

400 g (14 oz, 2 cups) basmati
  rice

1 litre (1¾ pints, 4 cups)
  stock or water (I like to use
  chicken stock)

1 bay leaf

salt and pepper, to taste

Preheat the oven to 180°C (350°F/Gas mark 4).

In a small casserole dish set over medium heat, melt the butter and sauté the onion until soft. Add the rice and stir to combine. Add the stock and bay leaf and season with salt and pepper.

Bake for approximately 20 minutes. When cooked, use a fork and fluff the rice up before serving.

Serves 4 as a side

Briam is a Greek version of ratatouille and is a dish of baked vegetables. It can be served on its own or as an accompaniment. Lamb goes well with it. I particularly love this dish served at room temperature.

Briam
Greek-Style Ratatouille

Preheat the oven to 180°C (350°F/Gas mark 4).

Place all the prepared vegetables into a baking dish. Add the garlic, oregano, thyme, parsley, salt and pepper and mix together. I like using my hands for this, but you can use a spoon, if you prefer. Drizzle over some olive oil and add 250 ml (8 fl oz, 1 cup) of water. Bake for about 1 hour, or until cooked. Keep an eye on it while cooking and add some more water if it starts to look too dry.

Serve hot or warm. Crumble the feta cheese over the top and serve with fresh crusty bread.

Serves 4–6

2 eggplants (aubergines), sliced
   into thin rounds
3 zucchini (courgettes), sliced
   into thin rounds
1 brown onion, peeled and
   sliced into thin rounds
4 potatoes, peeled and sliced
4 tomatoes, quartered
1 red capsicum (bell pepper),
   cut into chunks
1 garlic clove, finely diced
1 teaspoon dried oregano
½ teaspoon dried thyme
2 heaped tablespoons fresh
   parsley, finely chopped
salt and pepper
olive oil
water
150 g (5 oz) Greek feta
   (optional)

I first tasted these rissoles in Santorini where the tomatoes are full of summer flavour. When making these, use the best, ripest tomatoes you can find...delicious.

Santorini Tomato Rissoles

6 large tomatoes, peeled, seeded and finely diced

1 small brown onion, peeled and grated (shredded)

1 heaped tablespoon parsley, chopped

1 heaped tablespoon mint, chopped

1 teaspoon sugar

1 tablespoon tomato paste (purée) (concentrate)

salt and pepper, to taste

175 g (6 oz, 1½ cups) plain (all-purpose) flour

olive oil

In a large bowl, place the tomatoes, onion, parsley, mint, sugar and tomato paste and season with salt and pepper. Mix everything together then add the flour. Combine well. The mixture should resemble batter.

In a large frying pan, heat some olive oil, about 2 cm (¾ in) deep.

Using a tablespoon, drop spoonfuls of the tomato mixture into the pan to deep-fry. Turn each over once only. Each side should take only 2–3 minutes, or until golden brown.

Continue until all the mixture has been cooked. Remove with a slotted spoon and drain on absorbent paper.

Serve immediately. Perfect on a mezze platter.

Serves 4

These stuffed capsicum are very popular in Greece where the long green and red capsicum, known as bullhorn peppers, are preferred. I like the red ones as they are sweeter.

Stuffed Capsicum with Cheese

Prepare the capsicum by cutting off the tops and removing the seeds. Set the tops aside.

Stuff the peppers with some feta cheese and put the tops back on.

In a large frying pan, heat some olive oil and fry the peppers until golden brown, turning carefully.

Remove from the pan and place on a plate, season to taste.

Serve immediately.

Serves 4

8 small red and green long capsicum (bullhorn peppers)
400 g (14 oz) feta cheese
olive oil
salt and pepper, to taste

One of my many favourite French dishes is the pissaladière. This is my Greek twist on a French classic.

Greek-Style Pissaladière

Preheat the oven to 180°C (350°F/Gas mark 4). Lightly grease a baking sheet

In a frying pan, heat some olive oil and add the finely sliced onions. Fry until soft and lightly golden in colour.

Place the pizza base on the prepared baking sheet and top with the caramelised onion. Arrange the olives on top and crumble the feta cheese over the onion mix.

Bake for 15–20 minutes, or until cooked and base is golden around the edges.

Serves 4

1 tablespoon olive oil, plus extra for greasing

8 onions, finely sliced

1 pizza base

175 g (6 oz, 1 cup) black olives, pitted and halved

100 g (3½ oz) feta cheese

This delicate summer dish is lovely served with some natural yogurt on the side and a green salad.

Stuffed Tomatoes

8 tomatoes, washed

1 small onion, finely diced

1 tablespoon olive oil

200 g (7 oz, 1 cup) risotto rice

2 heaped tablespoons parsley, chopped

1 heaped tablespoon dill, chopped

1 heaped tablespoon mint, chopped

sea salt

freshly ground black pepper

Slice the tops off each of the tomatoes but retain them to use later as a lid. Scoop out the innards and set aside. Discard the seeds and chop up the flesh.

Sauté the onion in a pan with a little olive oil until soft. Add the rice, tomato flesh, herbs and season to taste. Cook for 5–6 minutes. Spoon the mixture into the tomato shells, put the lids on and arrange in an ovenproof dish. Drizzle with a little olive oil and pour about 250 ml (8 fl oz, 1 cup) of water into the dish. Bake for 45 minutes to 1 hour, or until cooked.

Serve hot with some fresh crusty bread.

Serves 4–6

I like to serve this dish with some Greek yogurt on the side. It is also delicious served with some Egg and Lemon Sauce (see Salads).

Stuffed Courgettes

Prepare the zucchini by washing and trimming off the stalk end. Carefully remove the pulp using a teaspoon or knife, to leave hollow shells, and set aside.

Place the minced beef, rice, tomato paste and herbs into a bowl and season. Mix well using your hands and fill the hollowed-out zucchini. Place the filled zucchini into a large pan, add 250 ml (8 fl oz, 1 cup) water and the reserved paste and drizzle with a little olive oil.

Cook slowly on the stove top, keeping an eye on it, for about 1 hour, or until cooked.

It's delicious served with some fresh crusty bread, or with some Greek yogurt on the side.

Serves 4–6

8 white (Lebanese) zucchini (courgettes)
200 g (7 oz) minced (ground) beef
5½ oz (150 g, ¾ cup) medium-grain rice
1 tablespoon tomato paste (purée) or 125 ml (4 fl oz, ½ cup) tomato passata, reserving 1 teaspoon paste (or 1 tablespoon passata) to use later
2 heaped tablespoons parsley, chopped
1 heaped tablespoon mint, chopped
1 teaspoon dill, chopped
salt and pepper
olive oil
Greek yogurt (optional)

Papoutsakia translates to 'small shoes'. This dish takes a little time to prepare, but is certainly delicious, served—of course—with a salad.

Papoutsakia
Stuffed Aubergine

4 eggplant (aubergines)

salt and pepper, to taste

olive oil

1 small brown onion, finely
  diced

1 garlic clove, finely diced

450 g (1 lb) minced (ground)
  beef

3 large tomatoes, peeled,
  seeded and chopped

1 teaspoon sugar

1 heaped tablespoon parsley

¼ teaspoon cinnamon

¼ teaspoon nutmeg

**FOR THE BÉCHAMEL
SAUCE**

50 g (1¾ oz) butter

50 g (1¾ oz) plain (all-purpose)
  flour

500 ml (17 fl oz) full-fat (whole)
  milk, warmed

1 egg

pinch of nutmeg

kefalotiri cheese, to serve

Slice each eggplant lengthways in half. Sprinkle the cut side with some salt and set aside for 20–30 minutes in a colander, cut side down, to drain.

Heat some olive oil in a large frying pan and fry the eggplant, for 2–3 minutes on each side. Transfer to a plate and allow to cool. Using a teaspoon, remove the flesh from the eggplant, being careful not to tear the skin. Chop the flesh and place in a bowl. Arrange the hollowed-out eggplant in a baking dish.

Using the same pan (you may need to add more oil) sauté the onion until soft. Add the garlic, minced beef, chopped tomatoes, salt and pepper, sugar, parsley and spices. Simmer for about 5 minutes then add the eggplant flesh and combine well. Fill the hollowed-out eggplant with the meat mixture.

Preheat the oven to 180°C (350°F/Gas mark 4).

To make the béchamel sauce, melt the butter in a pan and stir in the flour until combined. Pour in the warm milk slowly, whisking constantly. Add the egg, the nutmeg and season to taste. Stir until thick.

Spoon the sauce over the meat, smoothing it out. Grate some cheese on top. Pour 250 ml (8 fl oz, 1 cup) water in the dish. Bake for 45 minutes, or until cooked. Serve hot.

Serves 4–6

The sweetness of the braised leeks is a favourite taste of mine and together with the goat's cheese, it makes for a delicate and perfect tart.

Leek and Goat's Cheese Tart

Preheat the oven to 200°C (400°F/Gas mark 6). Lightly grease a tart tin (pan)

Roll out the pastry and use to line the tart tin. Using a fork, prick the base and then bake for 10–12 minutes, or until golden. Remove from the oven and leave aside.

In a large frying pan, heat a little olive oil over medium heat. Sauté the leeks until soft. Remove from the heat and tip into a bowl with the eggs, cream and seasoning. Stir well to combine and pour into the prepared pastry case. Dot with pieces of goat's cheese and bake for 20–25 minutes, or until cooked.

Serves 4–6

1 sheet shortcrust pastry
3 leeks, trimmed and sliced thinly
olive oil
2 eggs
200 ml (7 fl oz) pouring (single, light) cream
200 g (7 oz) goat's cheese
salt and pepper, to taste

Quiche is a classic French dish that we are all familiar with. I have used readymade pastry in this recipe, so it can be prepared easily and quickly.

Quiche Lorraine

Oil, for greasing

1 sheets shortcrust pastry

200 g (7 oz) thick-sliced bacon, trimmed and diced

4 eggs

125 ml (4 fl oz, ½ cup) crème fraîche

salt and pepper, to taste

Preheat the oven to 200°C (400°F/Gas mark 6).

Lightly grease a quiche tin (pan). Line with the pastry and trim the sides. Prick the base with a fork and bake in the oven for about 10–12 minutes, or until golden.

Scatter the bacon evenly over the pastry case base.

In a bowl, lightly whisk the eggs and crème fraîche using a fork. Season to taste and pour the mixture over the bacon.

Bake for about 20 minutes, or until set.

Serve hot with a green salad.

Serves 4–6

Roasted red capsicum have a delightful flavour. I love roasting a batch, dressing them and, after enjoying some, still having more in the refrigerator for the next few days. They will keep chilled for a week.

Preserving Roasted Red Capsicum

Preheat the oven to 200°C (400°F/Gas mark 6). Place the capsicum on a baking tray and roast until the skin has blistered and turned almost black, but not burnt. Remove from the oven and allow to cool. Cover with cling film or plastic wrap while hot so that the skin sweats. When cool enough to handle, unwrap, remove the skin and the seeds and slice the flesh into thick strips.

Place into plastic bags, remove as much air as possible and freeze. The capsicum will keep for at least six months.

Thaw when needed and dress with a drizzle of olive oil and vinegar, sprinkle with parsley, basil, garlic and seasoned well with salt.

Serves 4–6

8 red capsicums (bell peppers)

DRESSING

100 ml (3½ oz) olive oil

50 ml (1¾ oz) red wine vinegar

1 heaped tablespoon fresh parsley, finely chopped

8 basil leaves, torn into pieces

salt, to taste

2 garlic cloves, finely diced

These pickled vegetables are perfect on a mezze plate. It is something my mother would make regularly, especially the red capsicum stuffed with cabbage, that was her favourite.

Pickled Vegetables

¼ *cauliflower*

1 green capsicum (bell pepper)

2 red capsicums (bell peppers)

3 stalks celery

3 carrots

2 bay leaves

2 whole garlic cloves, peeled

FOR THE BRINE

115 g (4 oz, ½ cup) sea salt

225 g (7 oz, 1 cup) sugar

2 litres (3½ pints) white vinegar

250 ml (8 fl oz, 1 cup) olive oil

Prepare the vegetables by cutting the cauliflower into florets. Cut the capsicum into strips and remove the seeds. Trim the celery and cut into small pieces. Peel and slice the carrots. Put them all in a large bowl.

To make the brine, in a large pan, bring to the boil 2 litres (3½ pints) water, the salt, sugar and vinegar and simmer for 4–5 minutes.

Pour the brine over the prepared vegetables and allow to cool.

Transfer the vegetables into two sterilised jars, which will each hold 1 litre (1¾ pints), and pour over the brine. Place a bay leaf and a clove of garlic into each jar and seal with the olive oil. The vegetables will keep for 2–3 months. However, once opened, store in the refrigerator.

Serves 4–6

Pickled Red Pepper Stuffed with Cabbage

Prepare the capsicum by slicing the tops off and removing the seeds.

Fill them with the shredded cabbage, carrot, celery and parsley and place into a large bowl.

To make the brine, in a large pan, bring to the boil 2 litres (3½ pints) water, the salt, sugar and vinegar and simmer for 4–5 minutes.

Pour the brine over the prepared vegetables and allow to cool.

Transfer the peppers into two sterilised jars, which will each hold 1 litre (1¾ pints), and pour over the brine. Place a bay leaf and a clove of garlic into each jar and seal with the olive oil. The peppers will keep for 2–3 months. However, once opened, store in the refrigerator.

Serves 4–6

6 medium red capsicums (bell peppers)
½ small cabbage, finely shredded
1 carrot, peeled and finely grated (shredded)
1 celery stalk, trimmed and finely diced
1 heaped tablespoon fresh parsley, finely chopped
2 bay leaves
2 whole garlic cloves, peeled

FOR THE BRINE

115 g (4 oz, ½ cup) sea salt
225 g (7 oz, 1 cup) sugar
2 litres (3½ pints) white vinegar
250 ml (8 fl oz, 1 cup) olive oil

This classic baked beans recipe is lovely with the chorizo.

Baked Butter Beans
with Chorizo

450 g (1 lb) dried butter (lima)
  beans or 2 x 400 g (14 oz)
  cans butter beans
1 onion, finely diced
100 g (3½ oz) chorizo, sliced
olive oil
1 celery stalk, sliced
1 carrot, sliced
1 red capsicum (bell pepper),
  seeded and sliced
1 x 400 g (14 oz) can diced
  tomato
salt and pepper, to taste
1 teaspoon sugar
1 tablespoon parsley, finely
  chopped
2 bay leaves

If using dried beans, soak them overnight in a large bowl of water.

Drain and set the beans aside. Preheat the oven to 180°C (350°F/Gas mark 40.

In a frying pan, sauté the onion and chorizo for 2–3 minutes in some olive oil. Add the celery, carrot and capsicum and fry for a couple more minutes. Add the tomato and season with the salt, pepper and sugar. Add the parsley and bay leaves and combine. Pour into a baking dish and then add the beans, together with 250 ml (8 fl oz, 1 cup) of water.

Bake ifor about 1 hour.

Serves 4–6

On my last trip to France I stayed with some friends and I loved the way that they made a meal out of a pumpkin gratin served with a salad. It's a tasty, simple family meal.

Pumpkin Gratin

1 kg (2 lb 4 oz) pumpkin
  (squash), peeled, seeded and
  chopped
3 eggs
250 ml (8 fl oz, 1 cup) milk
250 ml (8 fl oz, 1 cup) crème
  fraîche
1 teaspoon sugar
1 teaspoon ground cinnamon
salt and pepper, to taste

Preheat the oven to 180°C (350°F/Gas mark 4).

Place the pumpkin pieces in a large pan of water and bring to the boil. Simmer until the pumpkin is soft. Drain well and mash.

Add the eggs, milk, crème fraîche, sugar, cinnamon and season to taste. Pour into a baking dish. and bake for about 30 minutes, or until golden.

Serves 4–6

When my children were small, the only way I could tempt them to eat cauliflower or broccoli was to smother it with cheese sauce. They are grown up now but still love this dish.

Cauliflower and Cheese Sauce

Preheat the oven to 180°C (350°F/Gas mark 4).

Cook the cauliflower florets in a pan of boiling water for 5 minutes, or until cooked but still firm. Drain well and tip into a baking dish.

In a pan, melt the butter then add the flour and stir well until combined and smooth. Slowly add the milk, mixing as you pour. Add the egg and cheese and stir until combined. The sauce will begin to thicken and resemble a custard consistency. Add the nutmeg and season to taste and then pour onto the cauliflower.

Bake for 20 minutes, or until golden.

Serves 4

1 small cauliflower, cut into
   florets

FOR THE BÉCHAMEL SAUCE

50 g (1¾ oz) unsalted butter

50 g (1¾ oz) plain (all-purpose)
   flour

500 ml (17 fl oz) full-fat (whole)
   milk

1 egg

50 g (1¾ oz) Cheddar cheese,
   grated (shredded)

salt and pepper, to taste

½ teaspoon nutmeg

A taste of the Mediterranean—I love these stuffed calamari.

Stuffed Calamari

4 calamari (cleaned)

olive oil

1 small onion, finely diced

300 g (10½ oz, 1½ cups) long-
  grain rice

1 tomato, peeled, seeded and
  diced

100 ml (3½ fl oz) white wine

salt and pepper, to taste

1 teaspoon parsley, finely
  chopped

½ teaspoon chilli powder
  (optional)

To prepare the calamari, cut the tentacles off and chop them into small pieces.

In a large frying pan, heat a little olive oil and sauté the tentacles with the onion. Add the rice, tomato and white wine. Simmer for about 6–8 minutes. You may need to add a little water if it is looking too dry. Season with the salt and pepper and add the parsley. Add some chili if you like a little heat.

Using a spoon, fill the calamari with the rice mixture until three-quarters full, (the rice will swell as it cooks). Secure the opening with a wooden cocktail stick.

Place the stuffed calamari into a baking dish and add 250 ml (8 fl oz, 1 cup) of water and a drizzle of olive oil. If you have any rice left, you can put that in the baking dish with the filled calamari. Cover and bake for 30 minutes, or until cooked.

Serves 4–6

These are a little fiddly to make but are worth the effort. This is perfect on a mezze platter or as a light meal. The stuffed vine leaves are excellent served with a dollop of Greek yogurt or simply a squeeze of lemon. You could also serve them with some Egg and Lemon Sauce (see Salads).

Vine Leaves Stuffed with Rice

To prepare the vine leaves, place them in some boiling water for approximately 2 minutes. Drain and remove the stalks.

In a frying pan, sauté the onion in a little olive oil until soft. Add the rice, tomatoes, salt and pepper and herbs. If you are using the pine nuts and sultanas add them now.

Pour in 250 ml (8 fl oz, 1 cup) of water and stir, cook for 7–8 minutes or until the water is absorbed.

To assemble, take a vine leaf and place, shiny side down, onto a plate. Place a tablespoon of mixture in the middle and fold over one end then fold the side inward. Roll all the way to the end. Place a few vine leaves in the bottom of a wide pot to cover the surface. After you've stuffed a vine leaf, place it in the pot, fitting them in snugly. When finished, pour in 500 ml (16 fl oz, 2 cups) of water to cover the rolls and drizzle with some olive oil. Place a plate over them to hold them in place and simmer on the stove for 1 hour, or until cooked. Add more water, if needed.

Serve warm with Greek yogurt or a squeeze of lemon.

Serves 4–6

450 g (1 lb) jar preserved vine leaves

1 small brown onion, peeled and finely diced

olive oil

200 g (7 oz, 1 cup) medium-grain rice

3 large tomatoes, grated (shredded)

salt and pepper, to taste

2 heaped tablespoons parsley, chopped

1 tablespoon fresh mint, chopped

1 tablespoon fresh dill, chopped

2 tablespoons pine nuts (optional)

2 tablespoons sultanas (golden raisins) (optional)

Greek yogurt, to serve

Lemon juice (optional), to serve

Italy is one of my all-time favourite destinations and I will never tire from visiting that gorgeous country.

I always wanted to see Venice and had the opportunity to do so in my last trip.

After dropping our bags at our apartment, we decided to explore—and the best part about exploring is getting lost. Just when you feel as though you're finally getting to know the streets, there is a new surprise waiting. It is the times when you are lost that you find that something amazing!

Without knowing where we were, we found ourselves at St Marks Square and stood there in wonder—I felt like I was in a dream. A dream may be the perfect way to describe Italy and all its hidden treasures waiting to be found.

I used to make this for my children as a way for them to eat zucchini. Now I make it as a light lunch served with a salad or as an accompaniment to a meat dish.

Vegetable Slice

1 kg (2 lb 4 oz) zucchini
   (courgette)
Oil, for greasing
4 eggs
125 ml (4 fl oz, ½ cup) milk
75 g (2½ oz) gruyere cheese,
   grated (shredded)
1 tablespoon parsley, finely
   chopped
salt and pepper, to taste

Trim the ends of the zucchini and grate the flesh coarsely.

Place in a colander and allow to stand for 15 minutes to drain. Remove from the colander and squeeze out any excess liquid. Tip into a large bowl.

Preheat the oven to 180°C (350°F/Gas mark 4). Lightly grease a baking dish.

In another bowl, beat the eggs, milk, cheese, parsley and seasoning. Pour over the zucchini and combine well. Pour everything into the prepared baking dish and bake for 30 minutes, or until golden brown.

Serves 4

Main Meals

Italian pizza is incredible. Toppings are minimal and bases are baked to perfection. My favourite is the very simple tomato and mozzarella pizza.

Pizza Dough

25 g (¾ oz) fresh yeast (or 1 sachet (7 g, ¼ oz) dried yeast)

1 teaspoon sugar

450 g (1 lb) extra strong white bread flour, plus 2 to 3 tablespoons extra

1 tablespoon olive oil

1 teaspoon salt

Place the yeast, sugar and 300 ml (10½ fl oz) warm water, in a bowl. Add 2–3 tablespoons of flour and beat to make a paste. Cover with a kitchen towel and allow to rest in a dry, warm spot in your kitchen.

In another bowl, place the bread flour, make a well in the centre and pour in the olive oil. Add the yeast mixture and mix until combined. You can add a little more flour or water at this point if you need to.

Turn the dough out onto a work surface, flour your hands and knead for about 8–10 minutes. The dough should be smooth and soft. Place into a clean bowl, cover with a kitchen towel and allow to rest in a warm place for 1 hour. It should double in size.

When it has risen, knead it again for a few minutes and then divide into three balls.

Lightly oil a pizza tray and roll out a dough ball to size. Place the rolled-out dough onto the tray, ready for the toppings to go on.

Makes 3 pizza bases

Main Meals

*This is a fabulous sauce for pizza. If you don't have fresh
tomatoes you can use canned.*

Tomato Sauce for Pizza Topping

In a large saucepan, sauté the onion and the garlic in the
butter and a little olive oil until soft. Add the tomatoes, sugar,
basil, salt and pepper. Simmer for about 20–25 minutes until
reduced and thickened.

Use this sauce as the base for your pizza, with a variety of
delicious toppings.

Makes about 500 ml (17 fl oz)

1 small onion, finely diced
1 garlic clove, finely diced
25 g (¾ oz) unsalted butter
olive oil
*1 kg (2 lb 4 oz) ripe tomatoes,
    peeled, seeded and chopped
    or 2 x 400 g (14 oz) cans
    diced tomatoes*
1 teaspoon sugar
handful fresh basil leaves, torn
salt and pepper, to taste

PIZZA TOPPING IDEAS
olives
*grilled (broiled) vegetables
    such as capsicum (bell
    pepper), zucchini (courgette),
    pumpkin*
anchovies
*meat such as salami,
    prosciutto, ham*
*Taleggio cheese (this cheese
    goes nicely with potato and
    caramelised onion)*
potato (thinly sliced)
caramelised onion
mushrooms

Tomato and Mozzarella Pizza

1 pizza base (see recipe)

4–5 tablespoons Tomato
    Sauce for Pizza Topping (see
    recipe)

4 fresh mozzarella balls

small bunch fresh basil, leaves
    picked

Make the pizza dough and tomato sauce, following the instructions.

Spoon about 4–5 heaped tablespoons of the tomato sauce on the pizza base. Tear or slice the mozzarella and arrange on the tomato sauce, together with some basil leaves.

Bake in a hot oven for about 15 minutes or until the pizza is golden and the sides are cooked.

Serves 4

Main Meals

Homemade pasta is heavenly. I remember my mother learning how to make her own pasta from her Italian friends. She bought a pasta machine and she even made her own lasagne sheets. The lasagne my mother made with her own homemade pasta was divine.

Homemade Pasta

Sift the flour onto the work surface and make a well in the centre.

Break the eggs into the well and add a pinch of salt and the oil. I like to use my hands but you can use a fork to stir some flour into the eggs. Keep adding more flour until it is all combined. Dust your the work surface with some more flour and knead the dough until it forms a silky ball.

Cover with a clean kitchen towel and allow to rest for 20 minutes.

If you have a pasta machine, you can use that, or if not, roll out balls of dough with a rolling pin and cut into shapes or strips.

Cook the pasta in a large saucepan of salted water for 4–5 minutes.

Serves 4–6

400 g (14 oz) 00 (super-fine)
  flour, plus extra for dusting
4 large eggs, beaten
¼ teaspoon salt
1 tablespoon olive oil

Lasagne is a great family meal. It takes some time to put together but the rewards are great. This is my version of this classic Italian dish.

Lasagne

1 large onion, finely diced

olive oil

2 garlic cloves, crushed

2 carrots, peeled and diced

375 g (13 oz) minced (ground) pork

375 g (13 oz) minced (ground) beef

680 ml (23 fl oz) tomato passata

125 ml (4 fl oz, ½ cup) white wine

1 tablespoon fresh parsley, chopped

1 tablespoon fresh basil, chopped

1 bay leaf

1 teaspoon sugar

salt and pepper to taste

250 g (9 oz) lasagne sheets

225 g (8 oz, 1 cup) mozzarella cheese, grated (shredded)

115 g (4 oz, ½ cup) Parmesan cheese, grated

FOR THE BÉCHAMEL SAUCE

100 g (3½ oz) unsalted butter

100 g (3½ oz) plain (all-purpose) flour

1 litre (1¾ pints) milk

1 egg

To make the meat sauce, in a large frying pan, sauté the onion in a little olive oil until soft. Add the garlic and carrots and cook a little more. Add both meats and fry until browned on all sides. Add the tomato passata and wine and stir. Add the parsley, basil, bay leaf, sugar and season well. Cover and cook gently for about 30 minutes.

Meanwhile, to make the béchamel sauce, melt the butter in a pan and add the flour. Stir well and cook for about 1 minute, then add the milk slowly, while stirring continuously. Cook on a medium heat until the sauce starts to thicken, then add the egg, mixing well. Set side.

Preheat the oven to 180°C (350°F/Gas mark 4).

To assemble the lasagne, pour about 3 to 4 tablespoons of the meat sauce into a lasagne dish. Arange a layer of lasagne sheets on top, then pour over one-third of the meat sauce. Drizzle one-third of the béchamel sauce over the top, then one-third of the mozzarella and Parmesan.

Place a second layer of lasagne and repeat the meat sauce, béchamel sauce and cheese layers.

Place a third layer of lasagne sheets on top and the remaining meat sauce then the remaining béchamel sauce and top with remaining cheese. Bake for 45 minutes, or until golden brown. Serve hot with a green salad.

Serves 4–6

I am sure that every household has their own version of Spaghetti Bolognese. This is mine—I hope you like it.

Spaghetti Bolognese

In a large pan, sauté the onions and garlic in a little olive oil. Add the mince and brown on all sides. Pour in the tomato passata, 375 ml (12 fl oz, 1½ cups) of water and the red wine and mix well.

Add the oregano, bay leaf and sugar and season to taste. Pick about eight basil leaves and tear into the sauce. Cook over low heat for 1 hour, keeping an eye on it and stirring occasionally. Add a little more water if it begins to look too dry.

When the sauce is almost ready, prepare the spaghetti. Bring a lalrge pan of salted water to the boil. Add the spaghetti and follow the cooking instructions on the packet. Drain the spaghetti in a colander, then pour back into the pan, add the butter and stir.

Divide the spaghetti between serving plates and, using a ladle, pour over the Bolognese sauce. Top with some grated Parmesan.

Serves 4–6

1 onion, grated (shredded)
1 garlic clove, finely chopped
olive oil
600 g (1 lb 5 oz) minced (ground) beef
680 ml (23 fl oz) tomato passata
250 ml (8 fl oz, 1 cup) red wine
1 tablespoon oregano
1 bay leaf
1 teaspoon sugar
salt and pepper, to taste
small bunch of fresh basil
400 g (14 oz) spaghetti
1 tablespoon butter
Parmesan cheese, to serve

Santorini, for me, is one of the most beautiful and breathtaking islands—there is no other like it.

On our last trip there, we decided to spend a day in Oia, for a little shopping, coffee and simply strolling through the cobblestone streets. After quite a bit of shopping it was time for lunch, so we asked some of the locals where we should eat. We were given directions to one of the most picturesque places in Oia, the port of Amoundi—this place has stayed with me since the moment I set eyes on it.

We had lunch in a taverna on the beach. Fish, of course, was on the menu, grilled and served with an olive oil and lemon dressing.

Our lunch came with a big bowl of Greek salad, roasted peppers, dips and lots of freshly baked bread to mop up all the juices, and a glass of wine—simply perfect.

We chatted with the owner, a gorgeous and generous woman, who came and sat with us. She told us about her life in the village and spending her summers at the beach looking after her taverna.

I think she had the best recipe for life.

Spaghetti Carbonara

400 g (14 oz) spaghetti
olive oil
6 rashers (strips) bacon or
    pancetta, sliced
3 large eggs
1 tablespoon fresh parsley,
    chopped
salt and pepper
100 g (3½ oz) Parmesan,
    grated (shredded)

Bring a large pan of salted water to a boil and add the pasta.
Cook following the instructions on the packet. If using fresh
pasta, cook for 4–5 minutes.

While the pasta is cooking, heat up a little olive oil and fry
the diced pancetta for a couple of minutes, or until golden.
Transfer from the frying pan to a bowl and set aside. In
another bowl, whisk the eggs, parsley, salt and pepper and
half the cheese. Add the pancetta.

When the pasta is cooked, drain in a colander and pour
straight into the egg mixture and stir well.

Divide on to serving plates, sprinkle the remaining
Parmesan on top and serve immediately.

Serves 4–6

Main Meals

Penne with Fresh Tomato and Basil

Put the tomato chunks in a bowl. Add the fresh torn basil leaves. Season with the salt and pepper and drizzle over a little olive oil.

In a large pan, bring plenty of salted water to the boil and cook the pasta until ready. Drain well and add the chopped tomatoes and basil to the pasta; combine well.

Divide into individual serving bowls and serve immediately. Some fresh ricotta or torn buffalo mozzarella will complement this dish.

Serves 4–6

6 ripe tomatoes, peeled, seeds
  discard and flesh chopped
1 handful fresh basil leaves,
  torn
olive oil
salt and pepper, to taste
400 g (14 oz) penne
100 g (3½ oz) fresh ricotta
  or buffalo mozzarella, for
  serving

Pasta is a regular family meal that I make when short of time. This is one of my favourite sauces.

Seafood Spaghetti

400 g (14 oz) spaghetti

450 g (1 lb) of seafood, calamari, shrimp and firm white fish pieces

1 garlic clove, peeled and finely sliced

olive oil

250 ml (8 fl oz, 1 cup) white wine

1 x 400 g (14 oz) can diced tomatoes

1 heaped tablespoon basil leaves, torn

1 heaped tablespoon fresh parsley, chopped

Cook the spaghetti in a large pan of salted water according to the packet instructions.

In a deep frying pan, sauté the seafood and garlic in a little olive oil. Add the white wine and tomatoes, stirring, and leave it on the heat for another 5–6 minutes, or until the seafood is cooked through, being careful not to overcook it.

When the spaghetti is *al dente*, drain it and pour it into the seafood sauce. Combine well, season with the salt and pepper and add the basil and parsley.

Serve immediately.

Serves 4–6

Pasta with Chorizo, Spinach and Red Onion

Bring a large pan of salted water to the boil, then add the spaghetti.

Meanwhile, in a frying pan, sauté the red onions in a little olive oil until soft. Add the sliced chorizo and cook for another 2 minutes. Add the sliced red capsicum and combine. Take off the heat and set aside.

Drain the pasta in a colander when cooked and pour back into the pan.

Add the onion, chorizo and capsicum. Mix together with the fresh spinach leaves and stir well. Season to taste.

Serve with freshly Parmesan cheese.

Serves 4–6

400 g (14 oz) spaghetti
2 small red onions, peeled and
  sliced
olive oil
200 g (7 oz) chorizo, sliced
2 roasted red capsicums (bell
  peppers), sliced
100 g (3½ oz) baby spinach
salt and pepper, to taste
fresh Parmesan, for grating
  (shredded)

Fresh zucchini, tomato and basil are delicious in this summery spaghetti sauce. Perfect with a generous dollop of fresh ricotta.

Tomato and Ricotta Spaghetti

400 g (14 oz) spaghetti or pasta of your choice
1 red onion, peeled and sliced
olive oil
2 zucchini (courgettes), finely sliced
4 fresh tomatoes, peeled, seeds removed and flesh diced
1 teaspoon sugar
salt and pepper, to taste
200 g (7 oz) fresh ricotta cheese
small bunch of fresh basil

Bring a large pan of salted water to the boil, add the spaghetti and cook according to the instructions on the packet.

In another large, deep pan, sauté the onion in a little olive oil. Add the sliced zucchini and sauté for another 2–3 minutes. Add the tomatoes, sugar, basil and season to taste. Add 125 ml (4 fl oz, ½ cup) of water and allow to simmer for about 10–12 minutes.

When the spaghetti is ready, drain in a colander. Turn the heat off the sauce. Pour the spaghetti into the sauce and combine well. Divide on to serving plates and top with a dollop of ricotta and a couple of fresh basil leaves.

Serve immediately.

Serves 4–6

Veal Ragù with Fettuccine

In a large pan, sauté the onion, celery, carrot and garlic in a little olive oil. Add the veal and brown on all sides. Pour in the tomato passata and 250 ml (8 fl oz, 1 cup) of water. Add 250 ml (8 fl oz, 1 cup) of wine, the bay leaf, oregano, parsley and sugar. Season well.

Simmer for about 1–1½ hours, keeping an eye on it and adding more water if it begins to look too dry.

When almost ready, bring a large pan of salted water to boil. Add the fettucine and cook according to the packet instructions. Drain and divide into individual plates and top with the ragù. I like to serve this dish with a generous amount of freshly grated (shredded) Parmesan cheese.

Serves 4–6

1 large brown onion, finely diced
1 celery stalk, trimmed and diced
1 carrot, peeled and diced
1 garlic clove, finely diced
olive oil
600 g (1 lb 5 oz) veal, diced
680 ml (23 fl oz) tomato passata
250 ml (8 fl oz, 1 cup) white wine
1 bay leaf
1 teaspoon dried oregano
1 tablespoon fresh parsley, chopped
1 teaspoon sugar
salt and pepper, to taste
400 g (14 oz) fettucine
Parmesan cheese, to serve

This risotto is perfect on its own or as a side to a meat dish. It is my Greek version of an Italian classic.

Risotto Avgolemono

1 small brown onion, finely diced

50 g (1¾ oz) unsalted butter

1 tablespoon olive oil

400 g (14 oz, 2 cups) risotto rice (I like to use Carnaroli)

1 litre (1¾ pints, 4 cups) chicken stock (I use a stock cube)

1 egg

juice from ½ lemon

100 ml (3 ½ fl oz) milk

salt and pepper, to taste

Parmesan, grated (shredded), to serve

In a large pan, sauté the onion in the butter and olive oil until soft. Add the rice and stir. Ladle in the chicken stock slowly, a spoonful at a time, and keep stirring. I usually use all the stock and keep an eye on it. You may need to add some water if all the stock iss absorbed before the rice is ready.

When the rice is cooked, turn off the heat.

In a small bowl, whisk the egg using a fork and stir in the lemon juice. Keep whisking, pouring in a splash of milk for creaminess and stir the mixture into the risotto.

Season to taste and serve with a generous amount of Parmesan.

Serves 4–6

Risotto with Asparagus, Peas, Mint and Parmesan

Trim the woody ends from the asparagus and wash the stalks well. Cut each stalk into three or four pieces and set aside.

In a large pan, over gentle heat, melt the butter and olive oil. Add the onion and asparagus and sauté until soft. Add the rice and mix well.

Pour in the wine and keep stirring until it has been absorbed, then add the stock a ladleful at a time. You may need more water or stock if the rice is not quite cooked before all the liquid has been absorbed. Just before the rice is cooked, stir in the peas and combine well, then sprinkle in the mint and season to taste.

Serve with a generous amount of Parmesan.

Serves 4–6

450 g (1 lb) asparagus
50 g (1¾ oz) unsalted butter
1 tablespoon olive oil
1 small brown onion, finely diced
400 g (14 oz, 2 cups) risotto rice (I like to use Carnaroli)
250 ml (8 fl oz, 1 cup) sweet or dry white wine
750 ml (24 fl oz, 3 cups) stock (I like to use chicken stock)
115 g (4 oz, 1 cup) peas (I use frozen peas)
2 tablespoons fresh mint, chopped
Parmesan cheese, grated (shredded), to serve

Paella is one of Spain's signature dishes. I love one-pot cooking and this is a great dish to serve to many people without doing lots of washing up.

Paella

1 onion, peeled and diced

200 g (7 oz) chorizo, sliced

olive oil

2–3 roasted red capsicums (bell peppers), sliced

2 garlic cloves, finely diced

pinch of saffron

400 g (14 oz, 2 cups) paella rice (I use bomba)

1 x 400 g (14 oz) can diced tomatoes

salt and pepper, to taste

125 ml (4 fl oz, ½ cup) white wine

1 litre (1¾ pints, 4 cups) stock

12 large shrimp (prawns)

150 g (5 oz) squid, cleaned and sliced into small pieces

150 g (5 oz) firm flesh fish, cut into pieces

2 heaped tablespoons fresh parsley, to garnish

1 lemon, cut into wedges

In a large paella pan, over medium heat, sauté the onion and sliced chorizo in a little olive oil, until soft. Stir in the red capsicum, garlic and saffron and mix well.

Add the rice and diced tomatoes and combine. Pour in the wine and the stock and bring to the boil. Simmer for 10–15 minutes, stirring as it cooks. If it is starting to look too dry, add some more water.

In the meantime, wash and prepare the seafood. Add to the rice mixture when the rice is almost cooked. The seafood should only need to cook for about 5 minutes until it is ready to eat. Sprinkle with the parsley, season to taste and serve with lemon wedges.

Serves 4–6

Main Meals

This dish can be made without the couscous and served as a mezze with some fresh crusty bread to mop up the juices. I like to serve it with the couscous as a main meal.

Youvetsi with Couscous

In a large ovenproof dish, sauté the onion and garlic in a little olive oil until soft.

Add the tomatoes, bay leaf, seasoning and the sugar. Simmer for about 15 minutes. Preheat the oven to 180°C (350°F/Gas mark 4).

Add the shrimp and combine well. Bake for about 10 minutes. Remove from the oven, crumble the feta cheese on top and return to the oven for another 10 minutes.

In the meantime, prepare the couscous by placing it in a bowl and adding 300 ml (½ pint) boiling water. Cover with a plate and leave for 5–6 minutes, or until the water is absorbed. Pour in a teaspoon of olive oil and fluff the couscous with a fork. Transfer to a serving plate.

Remove the shrimp dish from the oven, sprinkle parsley over and spoon onto a plateful of couscous. Serve immediately.

Serves 4–6

1 small onion, finely diced
2 garlic cloves, finely diced
olive oil
6 large ripe tomatoes, peeled, seeded and diced
1 bay leaf
salt and pepper, to taste
½ teaspoon sugar
12–16 shrimp (prawns), depending on size
100 g (3½ oz) feta cheese
300 g (10½ oz) couscous
1 heaped tablespoon fresh parsley, chopped

I make this dish regularly for my family as it's easy and full of goodness. Salmon is not found in the Mediterranean, but is still a favourite. Substitute the salmon for your favourite fish, if you like.

Baked Salmon with Rice Pilaf

4 salmon fillets, skin on

olive oil

1 small onion, finely diced

4 large ripe tomatoes, peeled, seeded and chopped

salt and pepper, to taste

1 teaspoon sugar

1 heaped tablespoon fresh parsley, chopped

Plain Pilaf, to serve (see Starters and Sides)

Preheat the oven to 180°C (350°F/Gas mark 4).

Place the salmon in a baking dish, skin side up, and pour 250 ml (8 fl oz, 1 cup) of water into the dish and drizzle some olive oil over. Bake for 20 minutes, or until the salmon is cooked.

Prepare the plain pilaf and place in the oven together with the salmon.

While the salmon and the rice are cooking, prepare the tomato sauce. In a large saucepan, sauté the onion in a little olive oil until soft. Add the tomatoes, salt and pepper, sugar and parsley. Add 125 ml (4 fl oz, ½ cup) of water if needed. Simmer for 15 minutes.

Spoon some pilaf on to plates, add a piece of salmon on top of the rice and pour some tomato sauce over the salmon.

Serve with steamed broccoli or a simple green salad on the side.

Serves 4–6

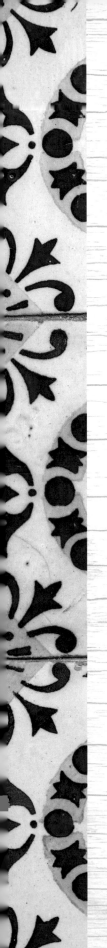

Salt cod is a favourite in Mediterranean cooking, which was a little surprising to me but it did make my husband very happy as it is one of his favourite foods.

Salt Cod, Potato and Tomato Bake

Soak the salt cod in cold water overnight.

Preheat the oven to 180°C (350°F/Gas mark 4). In a large baking dish, sauté the onion in a little olive oil. Place the potatoes in the dish, together with the tomato. Season with salt and pepper, add oregano and parsley and combine.

Remove the salt cod from the water and cut into individual portions. Add to the potato mixture and mix well. Pour a little water into the dish, drizzle with olive oil and bake in the oven for 1 hour, or until cooked.

Serve with a green salad.

Serves 4–6

450 g (1 lb) salt cod

1 large onion, peeled and finely sliced

olive oil

6 potatoes, peeled and sliced into rounds

4 tomatoes, grated (shredded)

salt and pepper, to taste

1 tablespoon oregano

1 heaped tablespoon parsley, chopped

In this recipe, I have chosen to use a whole snapper but you can use any firm-fleshed fish. You can also use fillets, if you prefer.

Baked Fish with Summer Vegetables

2 onions, peeled and
   quartered
2 garlic cloves, finely diced
olive oil
1 whole snapper, cleaned and
   scaled
3 zucchini (courgettes), cut in
   half and sliced lengthways
4 tomatoes, quartered
4 potatoes, peeled and cut into
   wedges
salt and pepper, to taste
2 tablespoons fresh parsley,
   finely chopped

Preheat the oven to 180°C (350°F/Gas mark 4). In a large, ovenproof casserole dish, sauté the onions and garlic in a little olive oil.

Place the fish in the centre of the dish and arrange the prepared vegetables around it.

Drizzle with some more olive oil, season and pour in 250 ml (8 fl oz/1 cup) of water. Cover and bake for 45 minutes, or until the fish and vegetables are cooked. Sprinkle with parsley.

Serve with fresh crusty bread so you can soak up the juices and a simple green salad.

Serves 4–6

Red mullet is very popular in Greece. It is a delicate and delicious fish, which is prepared simply. My mother always coated her fish with a little flour and fried it in some olive oil. This is the way I cook my fish also as I know that it always works and tastes great.

Pan-Fried Red Mullet

Pat the fish dry with kitchen paper and coat both sides with the flour.

Heat some olive oil in a large pan.

When the oil is hot, add the fish and cook for a few minutes on each side, or until golden, turning once. As this is a very delicate fish take care handling it.

Season with salt.

Carefully place onto a plate using a spatula and serve simply with an oil and lemon dressing or lemon wedges, a salad and some fresh crusty bread.

4 red mullet, cleaned and left whole (I also like to use snapper)

plain (all-purpose) flour, for coating (optional)

olive oil

salt, to taste

Oil and Lemon dressing (see recipe)

lemon wedges

Serves 4–6

When making the stock for this dish I like to make some extra to use for a soup. The Greek yogurt gives the chicken a delicious creaminess.

Chicken with Bulghur Wheat and Greek Yogurt

1 chicken, cut into 8 pieces, or
    8 chicken thighs on the bone,
    skin on
1 onion, finely diced
1 garlic clove, finely diced
olive oil
250 g (9 oz, 1½ cups) bulghur
    wheat
1 tablespoon fresh parsley,
    finely chopped
1 teaspoon fresh mint, finely
    chopped
Greek yogurt, to serve

Place the chicken pieces in a large stockpot and cover with water. Bring to the boil and simmer until the chicken is tender. Remove the chicken and set aside. Skim the stock and season with salt and pepper.

In a shallow casserole dish, sauté the onion and garlic in a little olive oil. Add the whole chicken pieces and brown on all sides. Add the bulghur wheat and pour in 750 ml (24 fl oz, 3 cups) of the stock. Put the lid on and simmer for 15 minutes, or until the wheat is cooked. Using a fork, fluff up the bulghur and sprinkle with the parsley and mint.

Serve with a side of Greek yogurt.

Serves 4–6

Main Meals

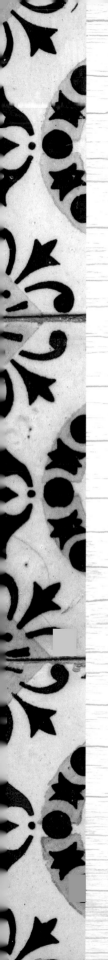

I particularly like making this dish with my aunt. When we cook it together, we pick the spinach and spring onions straight from her vegetable garden, so the vegetables go from the soil to the plate.

Chicken and Spinach Risotto

In a large pan, sauté the spring onions in a little olive oil. Add the chicken and brown on all sides. Add the tomatoes and rice and stir well. Pour in 500 ml (16 fl oz, 2 cups) of water and the chopped spinach. Simmer for about 15–20 minutes or until the rice and chicken are cooked. Keep an eye on it while cooking, stirring occasionally and, if needed, add a little more water.

Season well and sprinkle with the parsley. Serve immediately.

Serves 4–6

3 fresh spring onions (scallions), trimmed and finely sliced
olive oil
4 chicken fillets or thighs, cubed
3 fresh tomatoes, grated or 250 ml (8 fl oz, 1 cup) of tomato passata
200 g (7 oz, 1 cup) risotto rice
1 bunch spinach, chopped
salt and pepper, to taste
1 tablespoon fresh parsley, finely chopped

This classic French peasant dish from the Provençal region is lovely served with some buttered pasta, boiled potatoes or simply on its own.

Boeuf en Daube
Beef Stew

1 kg (2 lb 4 oz) gravy (stewing) beef, cut into bite-sized cubes
100 ml (3½ fl oz) white wine
olive oil
2 tablespoons brandy
salt and freshly ground black pepper, to taste
3 carrots, peeled and diced
75 g (2½ oz, 1 cup) mushrooms, sliced
1 brown onion, finely diced
4 rashers (strips) bacon, diced
85 g (3 oz, ½ cup) pitted black olives
250 ml (8 fl oz, 1 cup) tomato passata
500 ml (16 fl oz, 2 cups) beef stock
1 tablespoon parsley, finely chopped
1 bay leaf
½ tablespoon thyme
a couple of pieces of orange zest

Place the beef in a large bowl together with the wine, a splash of olive oil and brandy. Season with the salt and pepper. Mix well and place in the refrigerator, covered, overnight.

The next day, place the meat, carrots, mushrooms, onions, bacon, olives and tomato passata in a large ovenproof dish. Combine well and add in the stock and seasonings.

Cover and cook at 160°C (325°F/Gas mark 3) for 3–4 hours, or until tender. Keep an eye on it while cooking and if it is looking too dry add a little more water.

Even more delicious the next day!

Serves 4–6

The cassoulet is one of France's most well-known, hearty winter meals served simply with some fresh bread. A Toulouse sausage is usually made with pork, smoked bacon, wine and garlic. You can find the sausages and confit of duck legs at most continental delicatessens.

Cassoulet

Preheat the oven to 180°C (350°F/Gas mark 4).

Brown the bacon and onion in a large ovenproof dish in a little olive oil or the duck fat until soft. Add the garlic and stir.

Add the carrot, celery, thyme and flour, mixing well. Pour in the stock and wine together with the tomato paste and the beans. Season well and bring to a simmer for a few minutes.

Cover and cook in the oven for 1 hour. Take the casserole out of the oven and add the sausage and duck legs. Scatter over the breadcrumbs and return to the oven for another 30 minutes, uncovered.

Serve with a sprinkling of chopped parsley and some fresh crusty bread.

Serves 4–6

250 g (9 oz) bacon, diced
1 brown onion, finely diced
2 tablespoons olive oil or
*   2 tablespoons duck fat*
2 garlic cloves, finely diced
3 carrots, diced
2 stalks celery, sliced
1 tablespoons fresh thyme, finely
*   chopped*
1 tablespoon plain (all-purpose)
*   flour*
1 litre (1¾ pints) chicken stock
100 ml (3½ fl oz) white wine
3 tablespoons tomato paste
*   (purée)*
750 g (1 lb 10 oz) cannellini
*   (white) or haricot beans,*
*   soaked overnight in cold*
*   water*
5 toulouse sausages
5 confit duck legs
breadcrumbs, for topping
3 tablespoons fresh parsley,
*   finely chopped*
salt and freshly ground black
*   pepper*

I fell in love with Spain, not only the beautiful towns with their winding alleyways, but the amazing architecture and so many art galleries that I loved escaping into.

I always look forward to eating the local food and, of course, when in Spain I was looking forward to the tapas—small plates of very tasty morsels, prepared with passion.

I use the same vegetables in my Poule au Pot as the traditional dish, but here I add some cabbage, which is lovely.

My Pot au Feu

1 kg (2 lb 4 oz) beef ribs
6 cloves
4 garlic cloves, finely diced
1 bay leaf
4 carrots, peeled and cut in half
3 celery stalks, trimmed and cut in half
4 small onions, peeled and cut in half
3 leeks, trimmed and cut into three
4 potatoes, peeled and halved
½ cabbage
olive oil
salt and pepper to taste
1 heaped tablespoon fresh parsley, finely chopped

Place the beef ribs in a large pan and cover with cold water. Place over medium-high heat and bring to the boil, then turn the heat down and simmer slowly, skimming the surface of impurities regularly. Add the cloves and garlic, turn the temperature down and cook the beef slowly for about 1½ hours. Add the vegetables, olive oil and seasoning and cook for another hour.

Serve the meat and the vegetables on a large platter with some of the stock or on individual plates. Scatter over the parsley.

Any remaining stock can be made into a soup—simply add some tiny pasta and cook for a few minutes until the pasta is cooked.

Serves 4–6

I love these French classics—they make delightful family meals.

My Coq au Vin

1 chicken, cut into 8 pieces (or 8 thighs, on the bone)

1 tablespoon olive oil

75 g (2½ oz) butter

12 small onions, peeled

200 g (7 oz) bacon, diced

250 g (9 oz) small mushrooms

2 garlic cloves, finely diced

500 ml (16 fl oz, 2 cups) red wine

1 tablespoon tomato paste

salt and pepper, to taste

½ teaspoon sugar

1 bay leaf

1 tablespoon fresh thyme, finely chopped

1 tablespoon fresh parsley, finely chopped

In a large, heavy casserole dish, brown the chicken in the olive oil and butter. Add the onions, bacon, mushrooms and garlic and sauté for 3–4 minutes.

Pour in the red wine and add just enough water to cover the chicken. Add the tomato paste and stir well to combine. Season and add the sugar and herbs.

Simmer on a low heat for 1 hour, or until cooked.

Delicious served with some buttered pasta.

Serves 4–6

Main Meals

My Poule au Pot

Place the chicken in a large casserole and cover with water. Place on the heat and bring to the boil. Turn the heat to low and simmer for 10–15 minutes.

Place the vegetables around the chicken in the pot. Drizzle a little olive oil over, season and add the cloves, garlic, bay leaf and parsley.

Simmer for about 1–1½ hours, or until the chicken is tender.

Serves 4–6

1 chicken
4 carrots, peeled and halved
3 celery stalks, trimmed and
  halved
4 small onions, peeled and
  halved
3 leeks, trimmed and cut into
  three
4 potatoes, peeled and halved
olive oil
salt and pepper to taste
6 cloves
4 garlic cloves, finely diced
1 bay leaf
1 heaped tablespoon fresh
  parsley, finely chopped

My travels to Greece took me to countries near by—Italy, France and Spain—and my love for all things Mediterranean was sparked. When you know one country, the ones around it seem familiar in many ways.

This chicken casserole is best served with a simple rice pilaf. I love the full flavours from the paprika and chorizo—they remind me of Spain.

Chicken Casserole with Chorizo and Peas

1 onion, peeled and diced

100 g (3½ oz) chorizo, sliced

1 celery stalk, trimmed and
  diced

1 carrot, peeled and diced

1 garlic clove, finely diced

8 chicken thighs, on the bone

1 x 400 g (14 oz) can diced
  tomatoes

100 ml (3½ fl oz) red wine

olive oil

salt and pepper, to taste

½ teaspoon smoked paprika

1 teaspoon oregano

1 heaped tablespoon parsley,
  chopped

115 g (4 oz, 1 cup) peas (frozen
  is fine)

In a large casserole, set over a medium-high heat, sauté the onion and chorizo in a little olive oil. Add the celery, carrot and garlic and sauté for another 2 minutes.

Add the chicken and cook until it starts to brown. Pour in the tomatoes and wine, together with 250 ml (8 fl oz, 1 cup) of water. Season with the salt, pepper, paprika, oregano and parsley. Lower the heat and simmer for 45–60 minutes, or until the chicken is cooked. Add the peas and continue cooking for another 4–5 minutes.

Serve with Plain Pilaf (see Starters and Sides).

Serves 4–6

This is my version of a roast dinner when time is scarce - a perfect summer roast using fresh tomatoes.

Quick Roast Chicken with Tomatoes, Onions and Potatoes

Preheat the oven to 180°C (350°F/Gas mark 4).

Put the chicken thighs, onions, tomatoes and potatoes in a large baking dish. Drizzle some olive oil over, season with salt and pepper and sprinkle over the oregano.

Combine all the ingredients well (I like to use my hands to do this). Pour in 125 ml (4 fl oz, ½ cup) of water and bake for 1 hour, or until the chicken has cooked through.

Serve with a green salad.

Serves 4–6

8 chicken thighs (skin left on)

2 onions, peeled and chopped into chunks

4 tomatoes, cut into wedges

8 potatoes, peeled and cut into chunks

olive oil

salt and pepper, to taste

dried oregano, to taste

These meatballs are so tasty—serve with a green salad or some buttered pasta.

Chicken Meatballs

450 g (1 lb) minced (ground) chicken

50 g (1¾ oz) breadcrumbs

1 small brown onion, grated (shredded)

1 carrot, peeled and grated (shredded)

1 zucchini (courgette), peeled and grated

1 potato, peeled and grated

salt and pepper, to taste

1 tablespoon fresh parsley, chopped

1 egg

olive oil

Place all the ingredients, except the olive oil, in a large bowl and combine well. Roll into meatballs.

Heat a pan over a medium-high heat and add 1 tablespoon of olive oil. Fry each meatball for 3–4 minutes on each side, or until cooked through.

Any leftover meatballs will make an excellent sandwich filling the next day.

Serves 4–6

Main Meals

There are many versions of this dish in the Mediterranean, and this is mine—simple, healthy and tasty.

Lamb Casserole with Cannellini Beans

In a large, heavy casserole dish, sauté the onion, garlic and celery in a little olive oil. Add the lamb and cook until the lamb has browned.

Stir in the diced tomatoes and the tomato paste and pour in some water—enough to cover everything. Add the bay leaf and oregano and simmer on a low–medium heat for 1–1½ hours, or until the lamb is tender. Add more water if it starts to look too dry.

Once the lamb is tender, add the beans and parsley and season to taste. Simmer for another 20 minutes.

This dish will go very well with some rice or buttered noodles, to soak up the juices.

Serves 4–6

1 onion, finely diced

1 garlic clove, finely diced

*1 celery stalk, trimmed and
  diced*

olive oil

*750 g (1 lb 10 oz) shoulder of
  lamb, diced*

*1 x 400 g (14 oz) can diced
  tomatoes*

*1 tablespoon tomato paste
  (purée)*

1 bay leaf

1 teaspoon dried oregano

*1 x 400 g (14 oz) can cannellini
  (white) or butter (lima)
  beans*

*1 tablespoon fresh parsley,
  finely chopped*

salt and pepper, to taste

The Mediterranean kitchen is relaxed, seasonal and said to be the healthiest in the world.

During my travels, I have been inspired by watching families and friends gathering over long lunches, talking, laughing and enjoying food and company.

I particularly loved the small plates of food on offer—the mezethes of Greece, antipasti of Italy, hors d'oeuvres of France and the tapas of Spain. So many different tastes and, depending which country you were in, these small plates of delights and surprises were accompanied by either a glass of ouzo, wine or sangria.

Food for the body and soul.

Salads
and Dressings

A very simple salad, perfect as a side to grilled (broiled) meats or as part of a mezze platter.

Cabbage and Carrot Salad

½ small cabbage, finely
   shredded
4 tablespoons lemon juice
salt, to taste
3 carrots, peeled and grated
   (shredded)
6 tablespoons olive oil
2 tablespoons fresh parsley,
   finely chopped

In a large bowl, place the shredded cabbage and pour over the lemon juice and season with a little salt. Using your hands, mix well and set aside for 1–2 hours. The cabbage will soften in this time.

Add the carrot and dress with the olive oil. Taste for the seasoning and add more lemon juice or salt, if needed. Place in a serving bowl and sprinkle with the parsley.

Serves 4

Salads and Dressings

I often wondered what it must have been like for my parents to leave their families back in Greece and make a journey to a foreign country as many did in the 1950s.

My curiosity took me to my homeland, where I searched for answers about my family. Greece, of course, has a special place in my heart and always will. The bonds I developed with the people and the land are dear to me.

I fell in love with Spain, Italy and France—the charming villages and exquisite architecture. There were also the luscious food markets that inspire and the people who are so warm, friendly and welcoming.

I love all the tastes in this summer salad so I decided to put them all together. Perfect on a summer's day as a light lunch.

Summer Couscous Salad with Watermelon, Haloumi, Red Onion, Pomegranate and Mint

To prepare the couscous, tip it into a bowl and adding 150 ml (5 fl oz) boiling water. Cover with a plate and leave for 5–6 minutes, or until the water is absorbed. Pour in a teaspoon of olive oil and fluff up with a fork. Transfer the couscous to a serving plate.

Pat the haloumi dry. In a frying pan, heat some olive oil and fry the haloumi until golden. Set aside.

Cut the watermelon flesh into pieces and add to the couscous. Place the haloumi on top and add the mint leaves and red onion. Scatter the pomegranate seeds onto the salad.

To make the dressing, place the olive oil, vinegar, pomegranate syrup, honey and salt and pepper into a bowl and whisk to combine.

Dress the salad with the dressing, scatter with slivered almonds and serve.

Serves 4

150 g (5 oz) couscous
150 g (5 oz) haloumi cheese, diced
olive oil
½ small watermelon
small bunch of mint
1 red onion, peeled and sliced
1 pomegranate, cut in half, deseeded

FOR THE DRESSING

100 ml (3½ fl oz) olive oil
50 ml (1¾ fl oz) white wine vinegar
1 tablespoon pomegranate syrup
1 tablespoon honey
salt and pepper, to taste

slivered almonds, to garnish

Using the freshest zucchini (courgette) in this salad makes all the difference. It's perfect as a side to grilled (broiled) meats.

Fresh Salad

3 small zucchini (courgettes)

225 g (8 oz) cherry tomatoes

1 heaped tablespoon fresh
  mint, chopped

100 g (3½ oz) goat's cheese

**FOR THE OIL AND
VINEGAR DRESSING**

100 ml (3½ fl oz) extra virgin
  olive oil

50 ml (1¾ fl oz) white wine
  vinegar

salt and freshly ground black
  pepper, to taste

Slice the zucchini into thin rounds and place in a salad bowl. Chop the tomatoes in half and add to the zucchini), together with the mint leaves.

Make the dressing by mixing the vinegar and oil togethr in a small bowl and seasoning to taste. Pour the dressing over the salad and combine well. Crumble the goat's cheese on the salad and serve.

Serves 4

Salads and Dressings

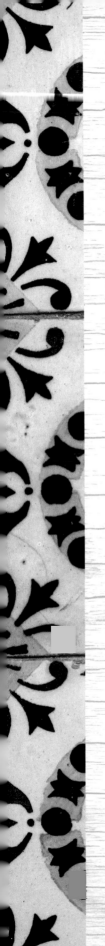

I love the sweetness of the peas in this salad together with the braised lettuce. Perfect as a side to roasts.

Warm Pea Salad

Melt the butter in a pan. Add the peas, lettuce and spring onions and combine. Add the sugar and 125 ml (4 fl oz, ½ cup) of water. Simmer for 15 minutes, or until the peas are tender. Season to taste and serve.

Serves 4

2 tablespoons unsalted butter

450 g (1 lb) peas (fresh or
　frozen)

1 small cos (romaine) lettuce,
　sliced

2 spring onions (scallions),
　trimmed and sliced

1 teaspoon caster (superfine)
　sugar

salt and pepper, to taste

Fresh mint or parsley, to
　garnish

We had a fig tree in our backyard when I was growing up. I remember my father picking figs for us. Most of the time the fresh sweet figs, still warm from the sun, never made it inside the house as we ate them straight from the tree.

My mother would often preserve the small, young green figs, if she remembered to pick them early enough. I still remember the jars that stood in her pantry—they gave me a reassuring, comforting feeling.

These are some flavour combinations I never tire of. You can prepare this salad ahead of time, leaving out the chorizo, allowing the salad to marinate. Then add the chorizo when ready to serve.

Tomato, Roasted Red Pepper and Chorizo Salad

100 g (3½ oz) chorizo

olive oil, for frying

4 tomatoes

2 roasted red capsicum (bell peppers), sliced

1 small red onion, sliced

100 ml (3½ fl oz) extra virgin olive oil

50 ml (1¾ fl oz) red wine vinegar

¼ teaspoon ground cinnamon

salt and pepper, to taste

2 tablespoons fresh parsley, chopped

piece of feta (optional)

Slice and gently fry the chorizo in a little olive oil in a frying pan set over medium heat.

To a large salad bowl, add the tomatoes, peppers and red onion.

Prepare the dressing by whisking the olive oil and vinegar together. Pour over the salad, sprinkle the cinnamon and season to taste.

Add the chorizo and sprinkle with the parsley. Combine all the ingredients gently using your hands.

Serve with fresh crusty bread. I like a little feta cheese with my salad.

Serves 4

The simplicity of this Italian classic is wonderful and for me can be a complete meal served with some fresh crusty bread. It's perfect for serving as part of a mezze too.

My Insalata Caprese

Onto a large platter, place the chopped tomatoes.

Tear the mozzarella balls into pieces and scatter among the tomatoes.

Make the dressing by combining the oil, vinegar, salt and pepper in a jar and shake until combined.

Pour the dressing over the tomato and mozzarella and sprinkle with the basil leaves. I like to combine all the ingredients with my hands gently and serve.

Serves 4

4 ripe tomatoes, chopped into chunks
4 rounds buffalo mozzarella
100 ml (3½ fl oz) extra virgin olive oil
50 ml (1¾ fl oz) red wine vinegar
½ cup basil leaves
salt and pepper, to taste

Mixed Greens Salad

1 baby cos (romaine) lettuce,
   outer leaves removed
3 spring onions (scallions),
   trimmed and sliced
1 small fennel bulb, sliced very
   finely
200 g (7 oz) rocket (arugula)
   leaves
200 g (7 oz) baby spinach
1 tablespoon fresh mint, finely
   chopped
1 tablespoon fresh dill, finely
   chopped
150 g (5 oz) walnuts, crushed
20 g (¾ oz) Parmesan cheese,
   shaved, to garnish (optional)

FOR THE VINAIGRETTE

75 ml (2½ fl oz) olive oil
2 tablespoons red wine vinegar
1 tablespoon lemon juice
salt and pepper, to taste

Prepare the dressing by placing the olive oil, vinegar and lemon juice in a jar and shaking until combined.

Arrange all the greens in a large salad bowl and dress with the vinaigrette. Sprinkle the walnuts over. Serve with some shaved Parmesan cheese, if desired.

Serves 4

Salads and Dressings

Tomato Salad

Chop the tomatoes into chunks. There is no need to be too precise about shapes as odd shapes can look lovely.

Peel and thinly slice the red onion and add to the tomatoes together with the basil.

Dress with the oil and vinegar and season to taste.

Serves 4

4 tomatoes (I like to use
    different varieties in this
    simple salad)
1 small red onion
1 heaped tablespoon fresh basil
    leaves, torn
olive oil
red wine vinegar
salt and pepper, to taste

I enjoy this classic French salad a great deal; it is one I make regularly.

My Niçoise Salad

4 tomatoes, cut into wedges

1 baby cos (romaine) lettuce, outer leaves removed

1 small red onion, sliced

2 potatoes, cooked and sliced

200 g (7 oz) green (French) beans, steamed or lightly boiled

4 hard-boiled eggs

115 g (4 oz, 1 cup) black olives

1 x 185 g (6 oz) can good-quality tuna in oil

4 marinated anchovies, sliced

FOR THE DRESSING

100 ml (3½ fl oz) extra virgin olive oil

50 ml (1¾ fl oz) red wine vinegar

salt and pepper, to taste

Place all the prepared vegetables, eggs and olives into a large salad bowl. Drain the tuna, break it up and scatter it and the anchovies onto the salad.

Prepare the dressing by combining the olive oil, red wine vinegar, salt and pepper in a jar and pour over the salad.

Combine gently—I like to use my hands to do this—and serve.

Serves 4

Salads and Dressings

It was market day in the village today so together with my cousin, who knew the market very well, we went shopping for the day's fresh fruit and vegetables. Today's lunch was going to depend on what the market had on offer. It is summer and the market stalls are filled with colourful capsicum, zucchini, tomatoes, green beans, cucumbers and much more. We decided on stuffed tomatoes and a salad. Watermelon was perfect for a refreshing end to our lunch.

While strolling among the market stalls I see that everyone seems to know each other. The Greek people will always wish you a 'good day' and 'kalo kalokeri' (have a good summer).

We arrived in Lyon, France, around lunchtime and our friends Brigitte and Adeline were waiting for us at the railway station. Brigitte had prepared a delicious lunch for us ready for when we arrived at their apartment. After a short rest we caught up over a lunch of pumpkin gratin and salad... simply perfect.

Les Halles de Lyon was definetly on my list of places to visit the next day. This indoor farmers' market is a foodie's haven. The stalls and produce are vibrant, the arrangements of sweets and fruit are presented like precious gems.

A stroll through the markets, for me, is a way of really getting to know a place and, of course, I always go home with some new and special finds.

This dish has become a favourite in our house. I think it is perfect on its own for a light lunch but you can serve it as a side to roasted meats for a more substantial meal.

Roasted Vegetable Salad with Bulghur

Preheat the oven to 180°C (350°F/Gas mark 4).

Place all the prepared vegetables in a large baking tray and drizzle with olive oil. Mix to combine and bake for 45 minutes, or until the vegetables are cooked but not too soft.

In the meantime, bring to boil a large pan of water to the boil and add the bulghur. Simmer for about 20 minutes. Drain in a colander and allow to cool.

Place the baby spinach onto a platter, place the vegetables on the spinach and then the bulghur. Dress with some vinegar, sprinkle with oregano and season to taste. Gently combine all the ingredients. I like to do this with my hands. Scatter the pumpkin seeds over and serve.

Serves 4

1 red onion, peeled and cut into wedges
2 garlic cloves, finely diced
1 sweet potato, peeled and cut into chunks
2 zucchini (courgettes), sliced thickly
2 red capsicum (bell pepper), seeded and cut into chunks
olive oil
150 g (5 oz) bulghur wheat
100 g (3½ oz) baby spinach
red wine vinegar
oregano, to taste
salt and pepper, to taste
75 g (2½ oz) pumpkin seeds

I made this salad for the first time with my aunt. The fresh sweet beetroot was from her garden, which made it taste special. The gorgeous colour of this salad looks perfect with some pistachios sprinkled over, so that is what I do.

Beetroot and Yogurt Salad

3–4 medium beetroot

125 ml (4 fl oz, ½ cup) Greek yogurt

1 tablespoon olive oil

1 tablespoon balsamic vinegar

¼ cup fresh mint leaves, chopped

1 garlic clove, finely diced

salt and pepper, to taste

30 g (1 oz, ¼ cup) raw, unsalted and shelled pistachios

Trim the beetroot and place in a large pan of water and bring to the boil. Simmer for 20–30 minutes, or until cooked. Remove from the water and gently rub off the skin. Cut into chunks or slices, whatever you prefer, and place into a bowl.

In another bowl, add the yogurt, olive oil, vinegar, mint leaves, garlic and seasoning. Mix gently and pour over the beetroot. Combine and scatter with the nuts.

Serves 4

This salad combines the fresh citrus taste of mandarin with some creamy goat's cheese and the fleshy sweet fig.

Salad with Goat's Cheese, Mandarin, Figs and Spinach

Place the spinach leaves into a salad bowl and top with mandarin segments and quartered fresh figs.

Prepare the dressing by whisking all the ingredients well in a small bowl, then pour over the salad. Top with pieces of goat's cheese and season to taste.

Serves 4

250 g (9 oz) baby spinach leaves
2 mandarins, segmented
4 fresh figs, cut into quarters
200 g (7 oz) goat's cheese
salt and pepper, to taste

FOR THE DRESSING

100 ml (3½ fl oz) olive oil
50 ml (1¾ fl oz) red wine vinegar
1 tablespoon Greek honey
2 tablespoons orange juice

This gorgeous lentil salad is perfect for a light lunch.

Lentil, Beetroot and Goat's Cheese Salad

3 medium beetroot

150 g (5 oz) lentils

1 leek, trimmed and sliced

olive oil

200 g (7 oz) goat's cheese

60 g (2 oz, ½ cup) walnuts,
  chopped

FOR THE DRESSING

1 tablespoon Greek honey

2 tablespoons red wine vinegar

4 tablespoons olive oil

1 tablespoon orange juice

salt and pepper, to taste

Place the beetroot in a pan of water and bring to the boil. Simmer for 20 minutes, or until the beetroot is tender. Remove from the water, gently rub off the skin and cut into chunks. Set aside.

If you are using lentils from a can, drain and set them aside in a bowl. If using dried lentils, wash and pick through the dried lentils before cooking. Boil the lentils in a large pan of water for 30–40 minutes, or until cooked. Drain and set aside.

In a frying pan, sauté the leeks in a little olive oil until soft.

To assemble the dish, place the lentils in a large salad bowl, top with the beetroot and sautéed leeks.

Make the dressing by whisking the honey, vinegar, olive oil and orange juice together and season to taste. Pour over the salad and combine gently. Crumble the goat's cheese over the salad and scatter the walnuts on top.

Serve immediately.

Serves 4

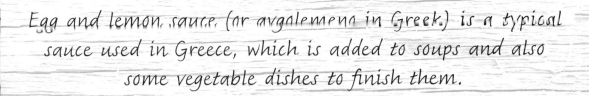

Egg and lemon sauce (or avgolemeno in Greek) is a typical sauce used in Greece, which is added to soups and also some vegetable dishes to finish them.

Egg and Lemon Sauce

Lightly whisk the egg white in a bowl, slowly adding the yolks and whisking a little more. Add the lemon juice gradually.

Slowly add in some of the stock or pan juices, from whatever dish you will be adding the Egg and Lemon Sauce to, beating all the time until completely combined.

Pour the egg and lemon sauce into the soup or over the dish.

2 eggs, separated
juice of 1 lemon
juice from stock

Oil and Lemon Dressing

100 ml (3½ fl oz) good quality
   extra virgin olive oil
juice of 1 lemon
¼ teaspoon salt
1 teaspoon oregano

Whisk the olive oil, lemon juice and salt in a small bowl; it should look a little creamy. Add the oregano and pour into a jar.

Store in a dark cupboard or the refrigerator for at least 1 month. Shake the jar before serving, to combine the dressing again.

Salads and Dressings

Salad Dressing with Pomegranate Syrup

Pour all the ingredients into a bowl and whisk well until combined. Season to taste and set aside.

I like to make this dressing fresh when I need it.

100 ml (3½ fl oz) good quality olive oil

50 ml (1¾ fl oz) white wine vinegar

1 tablespoon pomegranate syrup

1 tablespoon honey

salt and pepper, to taste

Salad Dressing with Honey

1 tablespoon Greek honey

2 tablespoons red wine vinegar

4 tablespoons olive oil

1 tablespoon orange juice

salt and pepper, to taste

Whisk all the ingredients well in a bowl, season to taste, and set aside.

Sweets

You will need a few large glass jars for this recipe. Once bottled, these make an excellent gift.

Apricots Preserved in Syrup

Pour 500 ml (16 fl oz, 2 cups) water into a large pan with the sugar. Add the apricots and lemon zest. Bring to the boil and simmer for 3–4 minutes. Transfer the apricots into large, sterilised glass jars. Allow the syrup to cool before pouring into the jars. Place the lids on.

Place the jars in a large pan of water, the water should come halfway up the jars, and bring to the boil. Simmer for 1 hour and then carefully remove the jars. The fruit should keep for several months in a cool, dark place. Once opened, keep in the refrigerator.

Makes 500 ml (16 fl oz)

1 kg (2 lb 4 oz) apricots

FOR THE SYRUP

200 g (7 oz, 1 cup) caster (superfine) sugar

lemon zest

I adore cooked apples, served on their own or with a rice pudding. You can adjust the sugar if this is too sweet for you, but I think it is just the right amount of sweetness.

Poached Apples

4 firm cooking apples

200 g (7 oz, 1 cup) caster (superfine) sugar

1 cinnamon stick

½ teaspoon vanilla extract

4 cloves

1 teaspoon lemon zest

Prepare the apples by peeling, coring and cutting into quarters.

Pour 500 ml (16 fl oz, 2 cups) of water and the sugar into a large pan and bring to the boil over medium heat. Add the cinnamon stick, vanilla, cloves and lemon zest.

Place the apples into the syrup and simmer gently for 10 minutes, or until the apples are cooked but still firm.

Serve with custard or Greek yogurt.

Serves 4–6

These oven-roasted figs are delicious. If you are too impatient and cannot wait for them to roast, you can have them fresh, served with ricotta and honey.

Oven-Roasted Figs with Ricotta and Honey

Preheat the oven to 180°C (350°F/Gas mark 4).

Prepare the figs by trimming the stems and cutting a deep cross into the tops.

In a baking dish, melt the butter and place the figs cut side up. Roast for 10–15 minutes.

Remove from the tray and arrange on a platter. Place a heaped tablespoon of ricotta into the cut cross. Drizzle with honey and sprinkle with some cinnamon and pistachios or crushed walnuts, whichever you prefer.

Serve immediately.

Serves 4–6

1 kg (2 lb 4 oz) fresh figs
50 g (1¾ oz) unsalted butter
250 g (9 oz) fresh ricotta
Greek honey
1 teaspoon ground cinnamon
pistachios or crushed walnuts

*My mother would often preserve small, young green figs.
These go very nicely with a coffee and a tall glass of
cold water.*

Figs in Syrup

1 kg (2 lb 4 oz) fresh figs (small,
   young green figs)
blanched almonds
450 g (1 lb) sugar
juice of 1 lemon
10 whole cloves

Wash and trim the stems of the figs and then pierce eacg fig
with an almond.

In a large pan, pour in 600 ml (1 pint) of water, the sugar,
lemon juice and cloves. Add the prepared figs, bring to the
boil and simmer for 20–30 minutes.

Carefully remove the figs from the syrup with a slotted
spoon and place into sterilised glass jars. Allow the syrup to
cool down, then pour over the figs in the jars until covered
completely.

Put the lids on and store in a dark place or in the
refrigerator. The figs will keep for up to 1 year. Once opened
keep chilled for upto several months.

These poached pears are full of flavour—serve with some Greek yogurt to balance out the sweetness.

Poached Pears with Vanilla and Honey

Peel, core and halve the pears. You can leave the stems on if you like.

In a large pan, pour in 500 ml (16 fl oz, 2 cups) of water, the honey, spices, vanilla and the lemon zest. Put the pears in and bring to the boil. Simmer for 15 minutes, or until the pears are cooked but firm.

Using a slotted spoon, take out the pears and place in a bowl and continue cooking the syrup for another 10 minutes so that it reduces. This is optional as you may prefer not to thicken the syrup.

Pour the syrup over the pears. You may like to drain the syrup first and remove the spices, but I prefer to leave them in.

Serve warm or cold with custard, yogurt or on their own.

Serves 4–6

4 pears
250 ml (8 fl oz, 1 cup) honey
1 cinnamon stick
6 cloves
6 peppercorns
1 star anise
1 teaspoon vanilla extract
zest from ½ lemon

I love making this chocolate tart as it is so simple and luxurious. It should be made using dark (bittersweet) chocolate but I prefer milk.

Chocolate Tart

FOR THE PASTRY

1 tablespoon olive oil

4 tablespoons water

1 tablespoon sugar

pinch of salt

90 g (3 oz) unsalted butter

*2 tablespoons almond meal
(ground almonds)*

*115 g (4 oz, 1 cup) plain
(all-purpose) flour*

FOR THE FILLING

250 g (9 oz) single (light) cream

*200 g (7 oz) good quality
milk or dark (bittersweet)
chocolate, broken into pieces*

1 egg

Preheat the oven to 200°C (400°F/Gas mark 6).

To make the pastry, place the oil, water, sugar, salt and butter into a heatproof bowl. Place into the oven for a few minutes, or until the butter has melted and the mixture starts to boil.

Take out of the oven carefully and pour in the almond meal and flour a little at a time, mixing constantly, until it has formed a ball of dough.

Place the dough on a board and knead it very lightly so it is all combined and then pat it into a 22 cm (8½ in) round tart tin (pan). Using a fork, prick the base, then bake for 12–14 minutes, or until golden and cooked.

To make the filling, heat the cream in a pan, over a low heat, and adding the chocolate pieces. Stir until the chocolate has melted. Turn the heat off and add the egg, stirring continuously. The mixture should start to look silky.

Pour into the prepared tart tin and bake for 15–20 minutes.

It tastes delicious with some fresh cream and berries.

Serves 4–6

My mother was a woman who always had a smile on her face and laughed at most things. Her laughter was infectious.

She was a beautiful woman who took pride in everything she did. My mother would rise early every morning so she could water her flowers and her vegetable patch and she checked on them again that night.

I loved the way she would prepare for her grandchildren whatever meals they asked for; nothing was ever too much trouble.

I still remember my children when young, their little faces covered in icing (confectioners') sugar when my mother would allow them to have kourabiedes (cookies covered with it) with a glass of milk for breakfast.

The sweets from Yia-Yia were precious.

They loved Yia-Yia.

*I adore this French classic dessert and to make life easier
I use ready-made pastry. Serve with ice cream, custard,
cream, or just as it is.*

Tarte Tatin

Preheat the oven to 180°C (350°F/Gas mark 4).

Peel and cut the apples into quarters andr emove the core.
Cut the quarters in half again.

In a baking dish set over gentle heat, melt the butter and
add the sugar, stir to combine and simmer for 1–2 minutes.
Add the apples and cinnamon stick and cook for another
2–3 minutes. Add the sultanas, if using them, and remove the
cinnamon stick.

Place the pastry over the apples and tuck into the sides.
Bake for 20 minutes, or until the pastry is golden and
cooked.

Allow to cool for a couple of minutes before turning out
onto a serving dish.

Serves 4–6

6 cooking apples
75 g (2½ oz) unsalted butter
100 g (3 ½ oz, ½ cup) caster
    (superfine) sugar
1 cinammon stick
75 g (2½ oz, ½ cup) sultanas
    (golden raisins) (optional)
1 sheet puff pastry

This is a refreshing and healthy breakfast, snack or dessert. I love the yogurt and honey together—it reminds me of days in Greece.

Melon Salad
with Honey Yogurt

115 g (4 oz, 1 cup) melon, watermelon, cantaloupe and honeydew, diced

115 g (4 oz, 1 cup) strawberries, halved

75 g (2 ½ oz, ½ cup) blueberries

½ lemon

500 ml (16 fl oz, 2 cups) Greek yogurt

4 generous tablespoons Greek honey

60 g (2 oz, ½ cup) raw, unsalted pistachios (optional)

Put all he fruit in a bowl and squeeze the lemon juice over. Stir to combine.

In another bowl, combine the yogurt and honey. Whisk gently to combine. Spoon the honey yogurt on top of the fruit. I like to finish off with a sprinkling of pistachios.

Serve immediately.

Serves 4

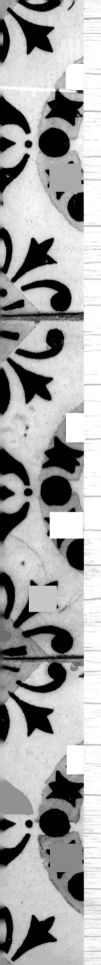

These crêpes are delicate and delicious. I like to have mine simply with a sprinkling of sugar and a squeeze of lemon.

Crêpes

In a large mixing bowl, sift in the flour. Make a well and add the eggs and beat using a fork. Add the warm milk, melted butter and sugar and keep mixing.

Using a crêpe pan or an oiled frying pan, pour in a ladleful of the crêpe mixture when hot. When the sides of the crêpe look golden and cooked, turn the crêpe over and cook the other side until golden. Continue until all the mixture is finished.

Serve each crêpe with a sprinkling of sugar and a squeeze of lemon or, as my family prefer, smothered with chocoalte sauce.

Stack the crêpes on a warm plate or serve each one immediately.

Serves 4–6

225 g (8 oz, 2 cups) plain (all-purpose) flour
3 eggs
500 ml (16 fl oz, 2 cups) full-fat (whole) milk, warm
30 g (1 oz) unsalted butter, melted
1 tablespoon caster (superfine) sugar

Many Greek desserts are made with syrup. This is a classic semolina cake, with the added flavour of coconut.

Coconut Semolina Cake with Syrup

250 g (9 oz) unsalted butter

200 g (7 oz, 1 cup) caster (superfine) sugar

6 eggs

250 ml (8 fl oz, 1 cup) orange juice

1 teaspoon vanilla extract

175 g (6 oz, 1½ cups) self-raising (self-rising) flour

175 g (6 oz, 1 cup) semolina

175 g (6 oz, 1 cup dessicated (dry, unsweetened, shredded) coconut, plus extra, to sprinkle

FOR THE SYRUP

300 g (10½ oz, 1½ cups) caster (superfine) sugar

6 cloves

a little orange zest

1 teaspoon orange blossom water (optional)

Preheat the oven to 200°C (400°F/Gas mark 6). Lightly grease a 23 cm (9 in) round cake tin (pan).

Beat the softened butter and sugar in the bowl of an electric mixer. Add the eggs one at a time. Slowly add the orange juice, vanilla, flour, semolina and coconut. Mix well.

Pour into the prepared baking tin and bake for 30 minutes, or until cooked.

Allow to cool.

To prepare the syrup, bring 750 ml (24 fl oz, 3 cups) of water, the sugar, a little orange zest and the orange water to a boil and then allow to simmer for 8 minutes.

Pour over the cooled cake and sprinkle some more coconut over. Cut into pieces and serve.

This delicious cake keeps well, covered, in the refrigerator for up to 1 week.

Serves 12

Kataifi was one of my father's favourite desserts. Whenever I see kataifi in a sweet shop it reminds me of him.

Kataifi
Nut Rolls in Syrup

To make the filling, combine the nuts and cinnamon in a bowl and set aside.

Take the kataifi pastry out of the packet and spread out onto the work surface. Divide into strips about 90 cm (35½ in) long.

Place a heaped tablespoon of the nut mixture at the top and roll all the way down to make a roll. Repeat this until all the nut mixture has been used.

Place onto a lightly greased baking tray, in rows, and brush or drizzle with the melted butter. Cover with foil and bake in an oven set at 180°C (350°F/Gas mark 4) for 30 minutes. Remove the foil and bake for another 15–20 minutes, or until golden. Set aside to cool.

To make the syrup, in a large saucepan, bring 500 ml (16 fl oz/2 cups) of water to the boil with the sugar, honey, spices and zest. Simmer for about 8 minutes.

Gently pour the hot syrup on the cooled rolls and when all the syrup has been absorbed arrange on a serving platter.

The kataifi will keep well, covered, in the refrigerator for up 1 week.

Makes about 20

1 packet kataifi pastry
   (available in continental
   delis)

FOR THE FILLING

*115 g (4 oz, 1 cup) walnuts,
   chopped*

*60g (2 oz, ½ cup) pistachios,
   chopped*

*60g (2 oz, ½ cup) almonds,
   chopped*

1 teaspoon ground cinnamon

*115–225 g (4–8 oz) unsalted
   butter, melted*

FOR THE SYRUP

*600 g (1 lb 5 oz, 3 cups) caster
   (superfine) sugar*

125 ml (4 fl oz, ½ cup) honey

6 cloves

1 cinnamon stick

1 tablespoon lemon zest

The bougatsa is a traditional Greek sweet, often eaten at breakfast—hot from the oven. This is heavenly on its own or with poached fruit. Best served warm and will keep in the refrigerator, covered, for 4–5 days.

Bougatsa
Filo Pastry Parcels with Custard

FOR THE CUSTARD

3 eggs

100 g (3½ oz, ½ cup) caster (superfine) sugar

175 g (6 oz, 1 cup) semolina

½ teaspoon vanilla paste

1.5 litres (4¼ pints) full-fat (whole) milk, warmed

FOR THE PARCELS

75 g (2½ oz, ⅓ cup) unsalted butter, melted, for brushing

1 packet filo pastry

icing (confectioners') sugar, for dusting

Preheat the oven to 180°C (350°F/Gas mark 4).

To make the custard, in a bowl, beat the eggs with the sugar until light and creamy. Add the semolina and vanilla and mix well.

Pour into a large pan and slowly add the milk, stirring continuously over the heat. The custard will thicken and be smooth. Set aside to cool.

Lightly grease a the cups of a muffin tray with some melted butter.

Cut each filo sheets and into 14 x 14 cm (5½ x 5½ in) squares. Gently place a square of pastry into a prepared muffin cup and brush with some melted butter. Repeat until you have placed four squares into each muffin cup. There should be excess filo, enough to bring together in the middle and press together gently, to make a parcel.

Place a heaped tablespoon or two of the custard into the filo cups, bring the filo together and pinch to close and seal. Repeat to use up all the filling.

Brush with some melted butter and bake for 20–30 minutes, or until golden. Remove from the muffin tray carefully and dust with icing sugar.

Makes 12